Leaders
BUILDING
Leaders

Discovering the How and Why of Leadership

by Kailey Marshall

DORRANCE
PUBLISHING CO
EST. 1920
PITTSBURGH, PENNSYLVANIA 15238

Dorrance Publishing Co
585 Alpha Drive
Suite 103
Pittsburgh, PA 15238
Visit our website at *www.dorrancebookstore.com*

ISBN: 979-8-8860-4121-7
eISBN: 979-8-8860-4786-8

Leaders

BUILDING

Leaders

Discovering the How and Why of Leadership

Dedication

This book is dedicated to my father who teaches me, my mother who supports me and my sister who challenges me to grow every day!

Contents

Introduction

As leaders we find ourselves wrapped up in so many decisions, projects, and issues that we often neglect to turn and look at those around us. A main ingredient to successful leadership is making the time to spend with your team. With so many competing priorities it is easy to see someone who, it seems, is handling things just fine and push that one-on-one just one more week, and then another, and then another. Before you know it, you have not set aside dedicated and uninterrupted time for your young leader for a whole month.

When this happens the next one-on-one often becomes just a catch-up meeting for everything that has happened over the month. An update on your team, outstanding issues, and anything that is the most pressing. Before you blink, it is time for your next meeting and your young leader walks out of your office with just as much pressure, stress, and no idea how they will keep moving another month until you have time to meet again. If we rush our young leaders and do not set aside the time to mentor them, then we are setting them up to fail. What is a leader if not someone who sets our people up for success and provides an environment where they can grow, thrive, and learn?

Throughout this book, we will discuss those areas that we think we do well, the areas we do not like to talk about, and the areas that we just need a refresher on. For young leaders reading this book you will receive a toolkit of how that you can carry with you on your leadership journey and share with the leaders that will eventually report up through you. Our jobs as leaders are not as much about gaining respect but giving respect and showing your team that they are your priority. With so many books focused on the why, and while we do discuss the why here as well, we will spend a great deal of our time talking about how.

We will be focused on the young leaders who have their first leadership role and those leaders who are guiding other leaders for the first time. This book is intended to challenge both the young and the leaders who have been in this game for a while but have never been given the how. We will spend our time creating a new mindset of how to think of ourselves as leaders and how we can interact with our staff and the other leaders in our organizations in a healthy and productive way. We will explore how to create an organization full of healthy leaders that will be the deciding factor of whether your business soars or simply exists.

When I was a young leader, why was always my first question so I could understand the process from beginning to end. However, the very next question to quickly follow was how. How am I supposed to get my staff engaged during team huddles? How am I supposed to know what formats to use or how the COO will want this report to look? How do I have a successful corrective action conversation with a staff member? How am I supposed to get my own work done with all these meetings? How do I rise above being just another peer and be a respected leader? How do I set my own priorities and those of my team? How could I possibly be responsible for creating a culture or be a decision maker when I don't even know what I am doing?

The first question we need to ask is how we define what kind of leader we are and what kind of leader we want to be. In our first chapter we will see just how many different articles and references to leadership there are out there. Do you want to be feared? Loved? Respected? Are you more interested in quality or quantity of your team's work? Most importantly, are you willing to work harder than ever before at a new level or are you going to simply stand on your title and lord over those that work for you? We will take the time to walk through how you even make this decision and what that decision will mean for your organization and your team. We will be looking through some use cases and examples of how to not only apply these concepts in our own position but how to teach the leaders under us how to apply them as well. Let's take this journey together and discover not only the why of being a leader but the how.

Chapter 1
What Is a Leader?

IF YOU GO TO GOOGLE AND TYPE IN "WHAT IS A LEADER" YOU WILL BE provided with somewhere around three million results. Everyone has their opinion on what a good leader is and how they comport themselves. Which way is the right way? What will be the most impactful for a young leader? Regardless of the level of leadership, they should be continuously striving to grow themselves and their leadership knowledge. Brene Brown says in her book, *Dare to Lead:* "A leader is anyone who takes responsibility for finding the potential in people and processes, and who has the courage to develop that potential." Whether we are a COO or a team leader, we should still be identifying those around us that have potential, and we are responsible for the growth and development of those who report up to us.

Management is a concept we are all familiar with. There is not a person in the world who has worked who does not have a horrible manager story. Managers clock your time, they focus on the job over the individuals, and they are often focused on only the bottom line. A leader makes the decision to focus on the employee first because they understand that a staff who has been set up for success and feels supported will always meet and exceed that bottom line. Building a strong company foundation begins with whether you have a team full of leaders or managers. Do your leaders focus on the growth of your people and company? Are they willing to be challenged and grow themselves? Or do you have managers that are great at meeting the bare-minimum numbers but have a high turnover rate of staff, are unwilling to listen to ideas and do not take the time to develop their staff but are constantly complaining about their team instead?

I have spent a great deal of my adult life applying two movie quotes to how I handle my entire world. The movies are extremely unlikely when you hear the titles as movies that would so drastically impact one's existence and yet when I heard these two lines I was forever changed. Something clicked inside of me, and I have applied them to my life ever since. In the movie *Australia*, Nicole Kidman's character is speaking with Hugh Jackman, and he says something along the lines of "That just is how it is." Her response changed my life. She responds with "Just because it is, doesn't mean it should be." For such a simple phrase let it truly sink in. How many times have you thought that your organization or situation could not change because it is what it is? Remind yourself, just because it is, doesn't mean it should be that way.

The second movie quote comes from an even less likely source for a life-changing quote. In the movie *World War Z*, Brad Pitt is running with his family from something they did not quite understand yet. At one point they are admitted into a family's apartment to hide for the night and rest. Even though the family offers to allow them to stay he encourages them to come with his family when they leave. To explain the importance between life and death he simply states, "Movement is life." Now I am not running from a zombie horde by any means, even though some days it sure feels like I am running for my life, but I am in the healthcare industry and so this has multiple meanings for me. Movement is life for patients, movement is also life for processes and organizations. If you are not willing to grow and move forward, then your company will stagnate. Have you ever seen stagnate water? There is life in it, but that life consists of parasites and anyone who drinks that water is likely to get sick.

However, if you are a leader who is constantly thinking through the concept of movement is life, then you will be at the forefront of your own personal growth as well as responding faster to growth that is needed in your organization and your team. Movement also means changing tasks and responsibilities as your organization grows. If you are the only one that knows how to perform a task, then your company's growth is subject to your limitations. Leaders make sure that their team has every tool they need to be successful with their main tool being knowledge.

On the opposite side, leadership does not mean sitting in your team's pocket all day. If you are a leader who is overworked, stressed out, working until 10 every night, and feels like you cannot trust your people, then you more than likely have a problem on your hands. While there are always times of growth where we put in extra time, and extra oversight, overall, we should build the team around us to be a team we can trust. Sheryl Sandberg says, "Leadership is about making others better as a result of your presence and making sure that impact lasts in your absence." Think through the past month, how many days did you dedicate to making those around you better? Does your team perform just as well when you are present and when you are not watching?

If your team cannot function without you there because they have no direction, then they are not functioning with you there either. The Oxford Dictionary defines "function" as something or someone that "works or operates in a proper or particular way." Or "fulfill the purpose or task of a specified thing." If we do not take the time necessary to teach our teams how to fulfill their purpose or how to operate in a particular way, then we will always be stressed, overworked and our teams will never grow. Another side-effect of this behavior is always having a high turnover rate. What does turnover rate have to do with it, you ask? Well, let's do an exercise that leaders should do way more often than we do: put ourselves in our staff's shoes. If you had a leader that was always in your pocket, refused to give you the information you needed to be successful and you could not perform your job without them right there, is that somewhere you would want to keep working? Is that a leader you would want to emulate and learn under?

We should be hiring people that are just as good or better than we are. Hire someone who will challenge you and do not be afraid to hire someone who might know something you don't. This is a scary concept, isn't it? I can just hear your thoughts: "But if I hire someone who knows something I don't then they will be a threat for my job." Truthfully, they might be. For a real leader, that should not create fear, it should ignite a desire to grow on your part. After all, if we never bring someone up behind us to take our job, how can we move on to the next one? We should have pride enough in ourselves and our position to want our staff to be that strong. While a good CEO understands the aspects of their organization and understands the general concept of how each department works, I guarantee they do not know how to do the individual job of the staff on the floor most of the time. Sometimes yes, maybe they have done it before. But as your company grows, that becomes less likely. We will discuss this in depth in chapters 8, 9 and 10.

Another representation of a strong leader is often to lead and direct, buffer and guide, but not to do the work themselves and not to always hold all the cards. A common issue that I have seen in the various organizations that I have worked with is that they hire people that will not challenge them, that they do not feel threatened by, and then they withhold information from anyone else in an attempt to maintain control or a sense of importance. How many times have you worked at an organization and there was that person who everyone had to go to because they were the only one that knew everything? Nothing was written down, no one else was trained on it and everyone was dependent on that one person for all the answers.

While that person might feel like this is job security or that it provides them with a sense of power or influence, all it does is cripple yourself and your team. If you are the only one that knows how to do your job, then you are the ONLY one who knows how to do your job. Vacations will either always be working vacations, or they will be stressful because you will be worried about what is happening back at the office or just visualizing the growing piling of work on your desk. There will be no sick days, no early days, and no free days. Even worse, your organization that you have spent so much of your energy trying to help grow will actually be failing and suffering because of your inability to train and share knowledge. If you ever decide to leave that position, then whoever comes behind you is destined to fail. At no point should there ever be just one person who knows everything. Encourage your young leaders to share their knowledge as well and it will become second nature to them.

There are too many wonderful jobs and pieces of the puzzle for everyone to understand the minutia detail of each role. Just think about the peace you would feel if you did not have to stand on top of your staff to make sure something got done. Think how much more work you could accomplish if you could pass off some tasks, meetings, reports, anything. It gives you room to tackle the next big thing headed your way. How can your organization scale if you alone carry the key of knowledge needed to take the next step?

I am reminded of a good friend of mine who had plants in pots around her house. One day I came over and all of the sudden the giant plant I had seen by the back door was much smaller and she had three or four new pots with new plants in them. I asked if the big plant had died, and she said, "No, it outgrew its pot, so I had to break it up and replant." The plant had grown as much as possible in the container it was in, with the boundaries it had, but when it was duplicated, when pieces of the plant were taken and put somewhere else, not only could that plant continue to grow, but it duplicated itself and provided new opportunities for a new plant to take root and grow.

The same is true of us. If we put ourselves in a box and do not allow ourselves to grow or stretch then, even though we might stay alive, we are stuck. If we take pieces of our day, though, and remove them from our box, we have room to grow again. If we take that piece we cut off or that we removed and put it in a new box and water it, it will also grow, and all of a sudden you look around and have accomplished double the amount of work. Your organization will be growing, and you will see the seeds of knowledge and wisdom that you planted throughout that growth.

On the opposite side of this coin, it does not mean standing back and pointing out flaws or propping your feet up and watching your team struggle with your expectations. Setting clear expectations is very important and we hear a lot about that in leadership training. However, there is a piece that we are missing. Setting clear and realistic expectations is that missing link. If the expectations make no sense, are not achievable, or are out of line for a role then we set our teams up to fail. If your staff has no idea why their process works as it does or the importance of how it was designed, they will be less likely to be wholly bought in. If your staff is not bought in to your process, then you will have an uphill battle on your hands that you will never win.

Throughout my career, I have worked in multiple positions and performed many tasks. My least favorite were the times that my boss clearly had no understanding of what it took to accomplish the task they set before me and set unrealistic expectations. It was unbearable to know I had failed before I had even started. Take some time with your teams and ask them what their expectations for themselves are. You will have a baseline and can challenge them from there. Make sure the expectations are clear and agreed upon. Ensure that the staff does not just nod their head but that they truly understand and can explain back what their expectations are. If they can adequately articulate their expectations, then you have already won your first battle.

This is where the extremely fun, and everyone's favorite part of leadership, comes in. Documentation. Yes, that is its own sentence. In many different industries there is an understanding that if it was not written down, it did not happen. HR cannot hold staff accountable for rules that they were never provided. A leader cannot hold their team accountable for a process that does not exist. Regardless of how many verbal conversations you have, write those processes, rules, policies, SOPs, and how-to documents down. Make sure that there is no one person, including yourself, that is the only person that knows something. Also make sure that the staff, or at least your youngest leaders or highest performing staff, get a chance to look at the documentation. Since they are the people performing the functions of that job daily, we should make sure it is appropriate and that your staff gets a chance to contribute. When they get to contribute then a new sense of ownership develops, and your team thrives.

Sounds simple, right? You would think so! After all, we have all done that job before, it is not that bad. We do that job every day and we know every nuance. The important thing to remember is your audience. Whoever is reading this will not have done this job every day and they will not know every nuance. Write the details out so that anyone could step in and understand the job and how to perform each task. We are talking about multiple month-long projects, sometimes a year depending on the size of your organization. Don't forget either that processes change, they must be updated, retrained on, and rolled back out. I can just hear some of you, "But wait, that is not my job! I am not supposed to be the one responsible for writing everything down!" Fair question, but here is another fair question. Who is responsible for the success of your team? If it is someone else, then perhaps you are in the wrong role. Do you have any information about processes that are not written down? Are you the only one that knows how to answer certain questions or process something? How many things do you understand and have a lot of experience with that you are expecting your staff, unrealistically to just know? As my father has told me, how is anyone supposed to know what they don't know?

Before you have a heart attack at the staff on the floor knowing how you determine which vendors to use or how to approve payroll, and how on earth you are going to have the time to get all of this done with everything else you have to do, remember, writing everything down does not mean that it must go out across the entire company. It also does not mean that it all must happen this week. As with everything else, prioritize which areas have the biggest need or hole in knowledge and begin there. Use this as an exercise for your young leaders, team leads, supervisors or those who desire a leadership role. Once everything is documented then it means that if you go on vacation then another leader can cover for you while you are gone. It means that if you decide to take that promotion or job offer that training your replacement becomes that much easier. We are accountable to our organization and team to make sure that this happens. This mindset of maintaining job security by withholding information is damaging to your own career and those around you. You cannot move up or on if you are the only one that knows how to do what you do. You might very well achieve job security, but you will also guarantee that you will not be able to grow either.

In my father's entire career, he was known as being steady, smart, organized, and an amazing mentor. At one point, he was tested to see how he handled stress. My father's test scores were ridiculous to think about for us mere humans. He was shown to handle situations with the same amount of calm and professionalism no matter how stressful they got. Regardless of the reactions of those around him, he was known for not losing his patience or his temper. How many people have been fortunate enough to work for someone like that? More importantly, how many of us, as leaders, could be categorized the same way? Usually a very small amount. In fact, he was tested not just in his organization, but against multiple national leaders and he was in the 1% of the nation's leaders who thought this way. This is huge! In a nation that has so many companies and leaders out there, only 1% of their leaders handled stressful situations the same way as they handled every other situation?

Let me ask you this, if you took this test, where would you fall on that scale? I know I would definitely not fall in the 1%. However, this is something to strive for. How many times have you seen a leader or been a leader who lost their temper or control in front of their staff? A general rule of thumb is to vent up and never down. Your staff should never hear you complain about another leader, process, or especially another staff member. We are all human and we all get frustrated and need a safe place to vent, but this should always be to your superior, HR, or your mentor. This should be lesson number one for young leaders. This is also sometimes the hardest lesson to learn but also one of the main things that can create dissention with your staff, fear, anxiety, or disrespect in your organization. This can be especially challenging if they were promoted from within a team to leading that team.

Going from being a peer to being a leader is one of the hardest transitions I ever made. Thinking that you had friends who would support you and then seeing the jealousy kick in or having to correct their behavior or work is hard. We need to take the time to teach how to do this. Take the time to do the first few corrections with them just watching. Let your team leads be the encouragement, positive presence, and excellent trainer on the floor. The worst thing we could do for someone who moved from being a peer to leading their previous peers is to just throw them in the deep end without teaching them how to swim.

Remember, a leader is someone that can see the big picture and provide direction for those that cannot see the forest for the trees. A leader is someone who guides those that report to them to their next destination on their career path. A leader is someone that makes the time and ensures that their team is their highest priority. Because a true leader is someone who understands if we do not support and mentor and make our people a priority, it does not matter what your big plans are or what the next project is. Our people are the cogs that make the wheel turn, and without them, just like that plant, we are stuck.

Chapter 2
Mentoring New Leaders

NOW THAT WE HAVE DISCUSSED WHAT A LEADER IS, HOW DO WE TEACH our new knowledge to someone else? For many leaders, it has been so long since you were a brand-new leader that it is easy to forget what it was like to step into that new role. The nerves and fears that came with the excitement and pride. We can easily look at young leaders and assume they know how to handle the little things. After all, we hired them for a reason, we saw something in them that showed their potential. Don't catch yourself with an attitude of impatience and assumption. Just because you know how to handle a certain situation, they probably do not.

Ralph Nader said, "The function of leadership is to produce more leaders, not more followers." If we want our leaders to be successful, we need to teach them how to lead. Not manage, but lead. Set them up for success by spending extra time with them in the beginning. Especially for someone who has never led before. Allow them to shadow you in some of your meetings that either you lead, or another leader that you respect leads. This lets them see what doing it right looks like. Have a prep meeting before that meeting to talk to them about how you decided the topics, who the audience is, how to create an agenda and how they should listen to the tone of the conversation.

After your preparation, let them sit in and observe while encouraging them to take notes over anything they have questions on. It is also good to prepare the others in the meeting that you are bringing someone new in ahead of time and what your intentions are for that individual. Once in the meeting, introduce your new leader to the other leaders and give them a moment to tell a little about themselves. Providing them the opportunity to be exposed to other leaders with different styles and personalities will do nothing but improve their skills. Throughout these interactions, your new leader should be paying attention to all the little details. How was the presentation put together, what was the flow of the meeting and how did they handle time management or conflict?

After this opportunity set aside a follow-up one-on-one within a day or two in which you can debrief your mentee. Ask their opinion, let them walk you through what they noticed and what impacted them the most. Encourage questions and for them to challenge the flow or layout of the meeting as this shows they are critically thinking. Answer any questions you can while also guiding them down the path of how you and the other leaders prepped for that meeting and what you got out of the meeting as well. This is twofold; you get to hear where your team member really is in their development, and you also give them the opportunity to start voicing and developing their own opinions. Walk them through what went well, what could have gone better, and ask how they can implement the same concepts with their new team. This will ensure consistency in meeting effectiveness across your organization.

Try to avoid providing the answers for your new leaders, leave space for them to speak and produce their own answers. If people can explain a concept, then they understand it, if they cannot explain it or teach it then they do not understand it. For those that are parents, this is something we do with our kids as well. Even though we like to think that we are extremely different as adults, we have the same wiring as children. As an example of this, for my children when we come across a dirty room, or dirty clothes on the floor or behavior that is out of line, instead of telling them what they did wrong, once they are old enough, we give them the opportunity to explain what they did wrong. We will ask, "Is that where your clothes go?" and the kids will respond, "No." We will then ask them what they should do next, and they will respond with the correct action.

After this, we help them walk through why they did not do the correct action the first time and how they can do better next time. This teaches them to think through their actions the next time and creates a long-term memory instead of them tuning us out. The same is true for our young leaders. Allow them the opportunity to walk you through what they think should happen in most situations and then course-correct as needed. When they get the answers right it will provide a feeling of success and pride and when they are wrong, they are in a safe environment to learn and grow.

If they have a team that they will be leading huddles or presenting in any meetings this gives them excellent exposure and is likely to jumpstart some ideas. Instead of asking your nervous new leader to start with a blank piece of paper, give them a template. If you have an agenda that you always use or a presentation template you always use, then make sure they have access to it. Assist them with putting together their first agenda and then have them practice that meeting or presentation with you ahead of time. This allows for the nerves to get out of their system so when they are standing in front of their unfamiliar staff, digitally or physically, they will be as prepared as possible. This is another example of providing consistency across the organization in meeting layouts, templates and company documentation.

It is not a bad idea to go with them to their first couple of meetings. Split the meeting up where you handle the introduction of the new leader, provide some company announcements, and handle any of the heavier topics. Then let your pupil step right up and walk through any training materials, reminders, set tasks for the team for the upcoming week, and talk through any great news or a core value of your organization. This takes the pressure off their first meeting and allows the staff to have an easy introduction to their new leader. During this time, though, make sure you are completely present. Sitting in a meeting with your team while you are on your cell phone the entire time or looking off at a different screen and not responding is counterproductive. You are showing your team that while you took the time to show up, they are still not your priority.

As a director in one of the organizations I worked in, I had one-on-one meetings with a COO. I was also given the opportunity to present in Director update meetings and even C-Level executive briefings. There was nothing more gutting than working on every little detail to ensure I had accounted for everything and was as prepared as possible and then watching my leader not look me in the eye one time but spend the entire one-on-one or executive briefing on their cell phone. This created a feeling inadequacy in me, it also made it very hard for me to maintain the desire to produce my best work when the leader was not even going to look at it. Your actions in meetings as a leader determine how your staff or young leaders walk out of that meeting. If you are engaged and communicative and provide a positive presence, they will feel that. On the other hand, they will feel it if you spend the meeting looking at your cell phone, looking bored, turning your camera off or even stopping and talking on your phone in the middle of the meeting. Even walking into a meeting with the best laid plans and great intentions can go horribly wrong if you have not paid attention to who your audience is.

In one of the Director positions that I had, one of my very first meetings with one of my teams went about as horribly as it could have gone. I did not get introduced to the team by anyone, so I just showed up in their weekly huddle and introduced myself. I was given a list of items to talk through with that team, but I was not provided any context. So, after introducing myself and beginning the meeting as I have everywhere else I had previously worked, what I did not realize was that I was completely shunning the supervisor who has been running those meetings. Instead of setting aside time for her to talk through assignments for the week, I set assignments for them based on the feedback I had received from the VP I reported to.

Unfortunately, that VP had never been to one of this team's huddles, they did not normally pay attention to their weekly assignments, and they truly had no experience with this team. This led to my insulting the supervisor, setting unrealistic expectations with my brand-new staff, and setting myself up as a tyrant who was out of touch with the realities of the position. After this, it took me six months and extensive one-on-ones, meetings with HR, excruciating conversations, and my having to come and apologize to my team before we began to make any real progress. Obviously, this is not the way I would have liked to begin. This impacted my own performance as I had been given expectations on what I should have been achieving with that team, and instead of achieving those goals, I was trying to repair my relationship with that group.

If I had taken the time to ask more questions instead of assuming I knew how to handle this meeting, if my VP had taken the time to understand what they were asking me to do and if we had all set aside time, in the beginning, to meet with the supervisor and just hang back in their first huddle, I would have saved myself six months and two employees. For those new leaders reading, this was after I had been in leadership for over eight years! There is always more to learn. The VP had an opportunity to learn in this situation as well, proving the point that no matter how high up you get in leadership, you will make mistakes. The difference between a leader that lasts and builds good leaders and a manager or leader that ends up damaging young leaders is their ability to learn from their mistakes and their ability to let their mentee watch and learn from their mistakes too.

This leads me to the next point that leaders would rather not do. Let your young leader see you fail. More importantly, let them see how you respond to failure. Your own, and your team's. When they forget to do something, or they mess up an assignment, take the time to walk them through the why and then how they can do it better next time. When you give them the confidence that they are not going to lose their job at the first sign of failure then you get a more confident and less tentative employee. They are more willing to bring you their mistakes or their fears and seek out wisdom and help. If your team members are walking around in fear of failure, then they are not going to give it their all.

Everyone reading, please take a moment and read this next line a few times:

Failure does not have to mean fear!

It does not have to mean that your young leader is paralyzed into inaction or even a knee-jerk reaction. We must teach them to take a deep breath in and a deep breath out every day, multiple times a day. Respond to situations instead of reacting to them and this includes moments of failure.

Take football for an example, if you are on the offensive line and are tentative what will happen? Your opposite defensive player will blow right past you and your quarterback will get taken out. If you are there with confidence, though, you are more ready and more focused on your assignment. If that same lineman has an instance where they do miss a tackle and make a mistake they must learn how to learn immediately and adjust. Instead of allowing themselves to fall into the quicksand of failure, they allow themselves to build a stronger foundation of knowledge. The same is true for your young leaders. If they are walking around gingerly or on eggshells at the fear of failure, then they have paralyzed themselves from success. If all you can see is fear, then you are not watching for the opportunities and focused on learning.

In the same thought process teach them how to handle their team's failures as well. Did you know how to have an effective corrective action conversation with a staff member in your first leadership position? More than likely not. We learn those tips and tools that make those conversations easier and more effective over time. For example, you should never write a staff member up without having a conversation with them about your concerns first. Many times, you find out that what you thought was a mistake was a misunderstanding. Going into those conversations it is best to have all your points written down, so you do not get off-topic. If you have specific examples of something they have done incorrectly have those examples pulled up to help them understand. We will talk about this more in a later chapter in more detail.

One exercise that I always use when teaching my new leaders is that they must pay attention to perspective. If you take a cup that has writing on it, it can be a tumbler or coffee mug, really any cup, and then hold it between you and your young leader, ask them what they see. Make them describe it from their perspective. What does the writing say? What colors do they see? Is there a lid? Do they see any ridges or a place to put a straw? Regardless of what they say your response is "I don't see that." They are going to look at you a little crazy and that is okay. Then you describe what the cup looks like on your side.

Now turn the cup around, same cup, it functions the same way, the side that you knew still exists but now you can see it from someone else's perspective. The value of this lesson is to make sure a young leader understands that just because they see it a certain way does not mean that their staff does. Make sure that you are showing your team your perspective and you are making a concerted effort to turn that cup and see the perspective of those around you. You could be surprised that neither of you are wrong and you might gain a new perspective.

The biggest piece of advice you can give your new leader, and often one of the hardest to learn, is how to control your responses. No matter who you are meeting with, what client you are talking to, or what the situation is, always deal in facts and not feelings. As leaders, our team will take their cue from us. If we are seen to panic, overreact, yell, embarrass or belittle people, then they likely have a staff that is rude to customers, a high turnover rate, and disrespectful staff. If, however, you remain calm, you deal in facts and not feelings, you handle correction in private instead of public and you shut down any overreactions before they can take hold with a calm response, you will find that you have a staff who is respectful, calm, happy and unafraid to bring forward any issues they have.

Throughout the rest of the book, each chapter will be dedicated to specific advice on each of these topics. The important thing for you to remember as a senior leader is to take your time. If you are not willing to spend the dedicated time at the beginning of a new leader's role, then you need to be prepared to deal with longer periods of failure. Like the six months that I spent correcting my report with my team, I created a much more difficult environment for myself and my staff. Even though I eventually built a good enough relationship with that supervisor to work effectively with them, I never fully had their trust and there was always a tense or formal relationship. We got work done, but I had lost the opportunity to try and teach or help her grow. Once she had seen me mishandle the first meeting and then watched me try to fix it, it was harder for me to reach her on a mentor level, and I ended up having to assign a different leader in the organization to be her mentor so she could still grow without my being a hindrance.

Know yourself, if you are not the best mentor for your new leader because you do not have the time to dedicate or because your personalities clash, or, as in my case, you start off on a bad foot but want to make sure they do not suffer from that, then set them up with another leader. If your organization does not already have a mentoring program, then just reach out to another leader that you respect. Even if you tag team and each take half of the time, then that staff member is still being supported, heard, and taught how. Too often we just give them the what. What their expectations are. What their job description is. What the makeup of their team is. What are the reports that are due? These are important pieces of information for them, but if they do not know how to handle these items, then we continue to set them up to fail. Let's set them up for success by providing them all the tools that they need, a toolkit full of how.

Chapter 3
Being Accountable

FAIR WARNING, THIS CHAPTER IS NOT AN EASY ONE. AFTER ALL, accountability of ourselves never is easy. But before you just skip over this chapter remember why you are here and what we are aiming to accomplish. True leaders that build true leaders that build true leaders. Step one to that equation is accountability.

As we discussed in defining what a leader is and how we then teach those ideals to our new leaders, one of the main topics we continually discussed was accountability. There are multiple types of accountabilities to address. Accountability of our team, accountability of ourselves, and accountability of our organization. If we are only willing to hold the staff on the floor accountable, which happens more often than any of us would openly admit, then you have a staff who is frustrated and a company that is stalled.

Throughout my career, I have never walked into an organization where this did not have to be constantly addressed. Why is that? Do we think that now we have made it to a level where we are no longer accountable? Is it just that we don't have someone looking over our shoulder for the first time in our careers or do we really have that big of an ego to think that there is no one else in the organization who could possibly know as much as we do so how could they hold me accountable? Think about that question hard before just providing the standard answer of "Of course I know I am accountable." Even at the middle management level, it is easy to get a big head and not think about what accountability really means. Remember, accountability is not just about meeting numbers or project deadlines, it is about knowing who you are accountable to and understanding that just because you are the boss, it does not mean your staff are not paying attention.

How many leaders have you heard make statements along the lines of "I do not owe them anything but their paychecks" regarding their staff? Or, "They have no business worrying about what I am doing, they need to focus on their own job." Sound familiar? Even if you have never said it, have you thought it? How often do you think that your work is more important than your team's work? How many one-on-ones or team huddles have you pushed because something came up, or there was an emergency, or you were running behind on a project?

I understand that emergencies happen and sometimes things are more important than a huddle. But the thing to remember is that your team are the cogs that keep the wheel of your organization turning. If you are not regularly maintaining and oiling those cogs, the wheel starts to shudder and then break. You will be dealing with many more emergencies if you do not take the time to handle your team. Prioritize, and always have your staff at the top of the list. Be realistic, is that emergency something that can wait 15 or 20 minutes for a quick huddle so you can hand out assignments? Is it truly something that will alter the course of the entire organization if it is not handled within 15 minutes or even 30 minutes? Sometimes the answer is yes and that is okay, but you need to make sure it is truthfully an emergency and not just an excuse to put off that huddle or one-on-one that you do not feel is that important. You also need to make sure that your staff is not left in the cold. Have a backup plan, even if it is another leader, rescheduling the meeting for later in the day or sending over your notes to the team lead to complete that one meeting.

Consistency is one of the biggest components of accountability. Accountability is a challenging thing to do. It is hard to be accountable and it is hard to hold others accountable. T. Whitmore said, "Admitting to a mistake means refusing to use other people as scapegoats to avoid responsibilities but rather courageously owning up to every single one of them." How many scapegoats have you used this week? How many times have you used an "emergency" to get out of a one-on-one or shifted a huddle because you were just not really prepared or even did not feel like it?

If we are not consistently meeting with our teams and providing them with updated information about what is going on in the organization, the status of projects, updated expectations, or, most importantly, providing that ear and uninterrupted time for them to voice their own questions and concerns, then we are doing them a disservice and are not the leaders we should be. Don't get me wrong, this is hard. Making the time to sit down and put together an agenda for a huddle, having to put down huge projects, massive numbers, and changing your mindset to get on their level are all challenging. I have had to walk out of difficult client meetings or CEO meetings and then walk right into a staff meeting and change gears to talk to my call center or billing staff on the floor. Those are completely different frames of mind.

It is so easy to look up and all of the sudden it is time for your next huddle, and you feel like you just had one. I have seen leaders across multiple organizations have huddles that became ineffective because they stopped being engaged and creative and I have seen huddles slowly disappear because the leader felt something else was more important. Yes, it is exhausting, yes, it will take everything you have, and if you want to be a good leader that builds good leaders, it will be exhausting. But it will also be extremely rewarding to you, your staff and your organization when you take the time to do it right. Be consistent in your huddles and one-on-ones, set your bullet points ahead of time so you do not forget any points, and have a decently regular tempo to your meetings, so your teams know what to expect. Keep notes during your one-on-ones so you know where to pick up. Take time to think through items that will be engaging. Think about who your one-on-ones are with and what their personal goals are and how you can help them achieve those. Is it having them read a young leadership book and discuss a chapter every week? Are you helping someone put together a presentation or teaching them how to have healthy conflict resolution between other departments in your organization?

The thing to remember is that if you hold yourself accountable for being consistent with your meetings and one-on-ones, you are setting that example for your team and young leaders as well. They feel heard and that they are a priority, you catch issues and problems much faster when you take the time to ask. I want to challenge you with something during your team huddles. Set challenges for your teams and for yourselves. For example, I currently lead five separate teams, during our weekly huddle I have two sections labeled "challenges." One is to discuss the status of last week's challenge and at the end of the call, we discuss their challenge for next week. This allows all the teams to hear the arduous work that is being done by everyone, it creates an environment where failure is allowed, and problems are solved together instead of hidden while also showing them that you are accountable to them.

You see, the challenge I am giving you in this book is to provide yourself a weekly challenge and tell it to your team. Maybe not all of them but produce a challenge for yourself. Even better, ask your team if they have any challenges for you. This could get remarkably interesting. Before you just shut this book and walk away let me explain the why. If you show your team that you can have a challenge set and hit it most of the time but also be able to walk in and say, "Honestly, guys, I missed my challenge this week, here is what I am going to do this next week to course correct and get back on track." They see what it looks like to be accountable, and they see what it looks like to admit a failure in a healthy way where they can pick themselves up and fix the failure instead of fall into the failure.

In every organization I have consulted with or worked at I heard the same thing when I spoke with the staff on the floor. They always felt like they were held to a higher standard than the leadership was. That they constantly were being written up or talked to about their job performance but that the leadership would walk around as if they never made a mistake and never got in trouble. Part of this, as we know, is that they are not in the meetings where we get it handed to us and we do our best not to show that stress or let that affect them. To counter that feeling, though, let's give them the opportunity to see us being held accountable, gasp, by them.

Another aspect of accountability for leaders is to make sure we are accountable to our staff and young leaders for providing them the tools they need to be successful. That is something we are accountable for. The entire purpose of leadership is to set your teams up for success and move roadblocks out of their way so that your organization can thrive. Whether we are developing the tools or not, we need to make sure they have their toolkit and manuals or SOPs to set them up for success. Remember this, you know the why and they do not always know the why. So, taking the time to give them the why and the how will ensure that your team is well prepared for anything that comes their way.

Think about it, from birth we need to be told the why. We are stubborn, so when our parents said do not touch the stove or the candle, most of us did at least once. Why? Because Mom never said why we should not touch it. Telling someone not to do something, with zero explanation, is as bad as putting a kid in a room full of cookies and saying do not eat any and then walking away. Even if they do not eat a cookie, we have created an unnecessarily stressful situation for them that did not need to be there. Give them the why! Whether it is that ego kicking in or the mindset that we are the boss, and they should just do what we tell them to do, I have found many leaders to get strangely irritated at the thought of having to explain anything to their staff.

And yet, when you are working with your superior, we want to know why. We might not ask it that way, it might look like this: "If we complete this project by that time how will that impact us as an organization?" "What are the risks or consequences of not meeting that deadline?" The word "why" is nowhere in those questions, but the answer to those questions provides us the direction and why that we need. We can put more of the pieces together because we see the entire picture and we have learned to critically think. Your staff on the floor has not been in the past six budget meetings or the leadership meetings. They do not understand the impact of their contribution or lack thereof. Does it really take that much more effort to give them the why?

Let me give you an example. In one of my roles as a Director of Admissions for five hospitals, I spent six months standardizing and updating processes. In that time, I made my staff move from having all their work on paper to going entirely paperless. Most of my team had been in their positions for 5 to 10 years, some of them longer. They had always used paper so what difference does it make? Well, we covered five hospitals, if someone were out sick or needed assistance because they had a huge influx of admissions, no one else could help them. At best they could go to someone else's desk and rifle through it until they found some form of documentation and then spend half of the day interpreting other people's notes and discovering where they left off. At worst the hospital suffered a horrible admissions day or someone had to drive to another hospital and try and find the paperwork necessary, which created huge delays.

If we standardized the process then no matter what hospital you were covering, no matter which physician you were working with, and no matter where you left off in your process, anyone, at any time could come right behind you and pick up where you left off. Sounds great, right? They should be thrilled that

I am making their lives so much easier. And yet there was resistance. The resistance came because I only gave them a cursory answer, which to the staff on the floor meant, "If I replace you, it will not be as difficult." Even though that is not what I said or meant at all that is how it felt to that team. For this reason, they were extremely slow to pick up the new process and standardize it.

About three months in I decided I was going to have a very harsh conversation with that staff. I had set the expectation, trained them, provided the SOPs, and even got the other hospital departments on board, what more did they want? Well, I found out. They wanted the why. In that week's huddle, I only had one agenda item, the new process. In that huddle, I asked one question: "What is it that you guys do not like or do not understand about the new process?" After quite a few hems and haws I took a different tack and said, "Okay, what is it that you are afraid of with this new process?" One lady, who had been with the hospital for eighteen years, said, "I am afraid that you will find me more easily replaceable, so I am trying to just keep my job." This is heartbreaking! I had added an extra three months' worth of stress on this team that they did not need and was not necessary because I did not take the time to provide the why.

So, I gave them the detailed why. I said, "Yes, it would make every one of you replaceable and that is the point. But not for the reason you are thinking. Who here has ever had a sick day?" Everyone raised their hands. "Who here has ever taken a vacation?" Again, everyone raised their hands. "So, while you are out, for the hospital and our patients to not suffer, then we need someone else in this organization and on this team to be able to replace you for that time. If you ever get promoted, we grow, or someone decides to move on to a different role, then it becomes quite a bit easier to fill in and train an inexperienced staff member. Do you find value in this?" After a minute they all looked at each other and finally came around to say yes, they saw the value in that. After that conversation, the team vastly improved and all of the sudden it all seemed to click. Once they saw how much more efficient it made their day, they all bought into the system and were actually excited about the new process.

What does this have to do with the accountability, you ask? Well, I could very easily have written up the entire team. They were not meeting the expectations that were provided and I could have "held them accountable" by writing them all up. Don't get me wrong, I am all for following procedure and writing up as necessary, but the first conversation should be just that, a conversation. Do they not understand a piece of the process? Is there an underlying fear that is holding them back? If you take the time to find out and then give them the why or how that will fix their issue, you have not only fixed a process, but you have bought loyalty with your team. After those verbal conversations and after we have ensured that we have provided all the tools and held ourselves accountable, it is here that we begin holding the staff accountable. If you have not provided the appropriate tools, training, conversations, and taken the time then this next part gets quite a bit harder.

Corrective action is difficult. So difficult, in fact, it has its own chapter in this book. There we will get into the nitty-gritty details of how to handle these difficult conversations and walk step by step through a few examples. For now, however, we are just going to discuss the reasoning behind holding staff accountable and what that looks like. How many times have you had a staff member that never seemed to have a good attitude, never hit their deadlines, and was never where you needed them to be? Most of us have had at least one staff member that pops immediately to mind. Maybe even a few staff members. Now, if we are all honest with ourselves, did we do everything we needed to do to assist in making that employee the best they can be? Did we follow appropriate HR guidelines for the write-up process, or did we just get irritated and either get "stuck" with someone or fire them without walking through the full process?

Accountability from a leadership perspective in a corrective action situation means taking ownership for our part, which includes consistently holding staff accountable. Not just when they REALLY mess up, or when we finally have had enough. But walking through a consistent and fair Human Resources process. Typically, this involves something like a coaching, verbal warning, first written warning, second written warning, a final written warning, and then termination. Within each of those steps is a clear conversation that is verbal and documented for clarity of the expectations and need for improvement along with an anticipated timeframe of improvement. There are always instances where termination is immediately appropriate, but make sure you have all of your documentation and that you are holding your entire team, and yourself to the same standard.

Do not get caught up in the trap of being afraid to write someone up because you do not want to deal with the confrontation. Elbert Hubbard said,

"The greatest mistake a man can ever make is to be afraid of making one." Staff is going to make mistakes and that is okay. If you go through the appropriate steps, then they will learn from their mistakes, and you will learn how to truly lead. Dealing with conflict in a healthy way is another characteristic of a good leader.

The last part of accountability I want to discuss is our accountability to our organization. We are accountable for the obvious things, of course, such as our clients, our staff and to providing quality work. However, there is more to it than that for a leader. We are also accountable for how we go about our work. Are we stepping on top of or in the way of other leaders? Are we always clamoring for attention or to be seen at the top? Or are we working together with our team to build a more superior product? If we take the time to learn emotional intelligence, then we reach a new level of accountability that is otherwise inaccessible to us.

How we respond, instead of reacting to our fellow leaders, clients, bosses, and staff will show our true character. Do we explode as soon as we are out of earshot or hang up the phone? Do we shake our finger in the face of our staff or use language that is, we will just say, less than professional? If we allow ourselves to deal in feelings instead of facts, then we are not holding ourselves accountable to our organization. I know this chapter is brutal! It is dealing with all those little things that we do not like to think about or admit about ourselves but are very quick to point out about another leader or our staff. This is challenging and this is taking it to the next level. If we can truly apply emotional intelligence and hold ourselves accountable to be consistent and available and present for our staff, then we will shine.

Accountability to our organization also means that we are not allowing our teams or our jobs to be at risk because of lack of documentation, lack of training or lack of staff accountability. Making sure that we are holding ourselves accountable for providing for backups and multiple people are trained on all processes should be a priority to prevent any risk to the organization if someone is out. I have seen this leave a company in a treacherous situation when they had employees be out for extended periods of time with injuries, sickness, or even vacations or leave the organization. If we do not realize that we have a team member that is the only person that knows how to do a task, then we are not taking accountability for ensuring the company is not at risk.

As I mentioned above, I know that this stuff is taxing! Leadership is not about assigning work or even writing your staff up and managing their time. That is what a manager does. Leaders wring themselves out every day to make sure that their entire team, and everyone on it, has all the tools they need to be successful. A real leader fights for their team and shields them from the wrath of superiors or clients. A real leader consistently shows up, has team huddles, provides direction and encouragement, and is a safe place to come to. How are you going to teach a young leader what it is to be a leader if you are not holding yourself accountable to the same standards you set for them?

If you hold yourself accountable and teach the leaders under you what accountability really looks like, and they follow that pattern and start teaching the leaders underneath them what accountability really looks like, then before you know it, after all the exhausting days and effort you will be a leader that builds leaders, that builds leaders and your organization will soar.

Chapter 4
Meetings, Meetings, Meetings

AFTER THE HEAVY TOPIC OF ACCOUNTABILITY LET'S TALK ABOUT WHAT most of us spend our entire day doing, bouncing from one meeting, to the next. At one point in my career, I was leading seven teams and going to 15 meetings a day. This meant that I worked 70–80-hour weeks because all my own work had to be done at the end of the day. I understand that many of you seasoned leaders will be nodding your head as if this should be perfectly normal. I am going to argue that it is not effective, efficient, or essential to have this many meetings or work this many hours every single week for our entire lives.

If we do continuously work 70–80-hour weeks, that is what we will miss, our entire lives. Your children's recital or game, an anniversary or birthday, funerals, vacations, or even just a simple movie night with friends or family. Humans are social creatures, but we cannot count meetings as our entire social quota for the day and think that is healthy. Building a report at 10:30 at night after a day of 15 meetings and two staff calls followed by catch-up meetings with the COO and CEO and checking your team's work for the day? How does that report look? How much longer does it take to put together because you are a shell of yourself by this point? How many errors do you spend the next day fixing or does your boss find because you were too fuzzy to catch them all? The odds are pretty high that the errors were high, it took longer, and that it is not your best work. I know, I have been there. I am still there sometimes! This is not to say that every single day you should log off at 5 P.M. and call it a day. But there should be a balance between work life and home life. One of the first places you can start is with meetings.

If I had a dollar for every meeting that I sat through and thought, what is the point of this meeting? Or a meeting that I walked away from with no answers... but more meetings scheduled, then I could retire right now. Not quite, but my 401(k) would be much healthier, and all my debt would be paid off. Regardless, I believe we can all agree that much of our days are filled up with meetings after meetings after meetings. Many of them run over, there are no agendas or follow-up documentation and even if it is a productive meeting, we find that we often come back later and realize that the people we were meeting with had an entirely different interpretation of what we discussed. This, of course, does only one thing, create another meeting to discuss the previous meeting so we can get ready for the next meeting.

Are you tired yet? Me too.

So how do we solve this as leaders? I mean, these are things that must be discussed, right? Decisions must be made and unless you are working in an organization that is tyrannical then multiple people need to be involved in some of the decision-making processes. Create an agenda, have specific bullet points, and then add notes as the call moves forward. Earlier I discussed my team huddle and how we had challenge sections. The entire meeting agenda flows like this:

Great News! — 5 minutes

- This is an area where anyone on the meeting has a chance to share something positive, either at work or personally, so we can celebrate the good things.

Core Value — 5 minutes

- We have 6 core values in my current organization, and we really mean core. We take a core value every single week and discuss it with the staff. How have they embodied this core value, or have they seen someone else in the organization display an excellent example of one of our core values, even what it means to them.

Previous Week's Challenge — 10 minutes

- Get an update from each staff member or group on how their challenge went from the week before. If they hit it or beat it then celebrate and if they didn't talk briefly about why and how we can adjust during the next week.

COMPANY ANNOUNCEMENTS — 5 MINUTES

- Announce any cascading messages from the organization.

OUTSTANDING TOPICS OR ISSUES — 30 MINUTES

- This is where you allow the team to come forward and discuss any issues they are having or anything they would like clarification on. This is the back-and-forth working session piece of the meeting.

NEXT WEEK'S CHALLENGES — 5 MINUTES

- Walk through quickly what that team or individual's challenge for the next week is and make sure that they thoroughly understand the request.

This is, of course, a simple example and will not be appropriate for every group or team. Whether it is this format, something similar, or using the Level 10 format from EOS, having a set agenda that is consistent and flows is essential. Having someone that truly leads the meeting and remembering to watch tone is also key. Whether in person or digital, tone matters. If the meeting is on Teams or Zoom, have your team turn their cameras on. So much of what we communicate is in our facial expressions and body language.

You can avoid a great deal of miscommunication and misunderstandings with your team by paying attention to your tone and using your body language and facial expressions. Making sure that we are teaching our young leaders to watch their own faces and hear themselves when they speak is extremely important. I have had so many first-time leaders that will take over their first huddle and come across one of two ways: extremely harsh and severe or just a friend. Neither of these is appropriate and yet, if we do not take the time to teach them how to handle a meeting then they will only learn through trial and error.

Another aspect of our meetings to think about is the staff involved. Is everyone in the meeting truly there because they need to be? Or are there people in the meeting who just like to be involved? We have all worked with and sometimes been that person who wanted to be involved in a meeting or process that was not really ours to handle but we wanted to have a say. We need to make sure we are efficient and effective with our time. This means being honest with ourselves and letting certain things go that are not ours to own. We

CLASSIC MEETING AGENDA TEMPLATE

DATE

00/00/0000

LOCATION

TIME

11:30 AM

TITLE

AGENDA DETAILS

I. **Agenda Item 1 description**
   a. Remarks
   b. Remarks
   c. Remarks

II. **Agenda Item 2 description**
   a. Remarks
   b. Remarks

III. **Agenda Item 3 description**
   a. Remarks
   b. Remarks
   c. Remarks

IV. **Agenda Item 4 description**
   a. Remarks
   b. Remarks
      i. Remarks
      ii. Remarks
      iii. Remarks
      iv. Remarks

V. **Agenda Item 5 description**
   a. Remarks
   b. Remarks
   c. Remarks

VI. **Agenda Item 6 description**
   a. Remarks
      i. Remarks
      ii. Remarks
      iii. Remarks

can jump into a kickoff call or ask for an update or even offer advice, but we have all been in the meetings where we have too many cooks in a kitchen. Make sure that we are not adding ourselves to meetings to feel important or because we want to have our name on that project but because it truly impacts us or if we can truthfully provide meaningful insight that others in the call do not have.

Within these meetings, use those agendas and set a timer, stay on track, and spend less time talking about the game last night or the vacation you are about to take. Being present is imperative during these meetings. There is always more work to do but stay off your phone and off your computer and be present during the meetings. Give the others in the meeting the respect of showing up mentally as well as physically. During these conversations, we must remember the intent of the meeting. If there is no intent or goal for that meeting, ask yourself if that meeting is necessary. If nothing is getting accomplished, then it needs to be reevaluated for necessity and content. There is no point in a meeting where the only thing accomplished is creating excess stress and frustration as well as wasting the time of those involved.

Before you get too excited, this does not mean just go cancel all your meetings. This means to evaluate your meetings and those involved as well as the intention and agendas of each meeting. At the end of this evaluation, I guarantee you will find meetings that are unnecessary, staff members being included that do not need to be, and agendas or intentions that need to be adjusted. This can help you get away from the meetings about the concept of the meeting we discussed previously.

The agendas and accountability within the meetings mean that we should be accountable to each other to remain professional. I have been in meetings where multiple people rolled back away from the conference room table to get out of the line of fire from two other leaders who were screaming, cussing, and doing nothing except creating more issues the entire meeting. The only thing accomplished in these meetings was more discord, more questions, and a lot of uncomfortable employees. This is an excellent example of where those leaders should have had much greater emotional intelligence and dealt in facts instead of feelings. Listen with the intent to understand instead of the intent to respond. If we can each do this and remain on track with the agenda, then we have an incredibly good chance of being productive in our meetings.

Just imagine, setting aside a block of time daily and weekly for work and focused time for yourself where you can accomplish your work, during the day, when your mind is fresh and focused. You now have time to do this because you are not bombarded from meeting to meeting every single day and the meetings that you are going to are productive, effective, and efficiently run. Your stress level could drop a little, and your own work will be more accurate, professional and take less time. Let's take our meeting madness days down to meetings that are useful and solve the issues that are outstanding.

How much faster would your organization grow if every single meeting were effective, issues were solved, minimal offline meetings had to be scheduled and the participants in the meeting truly needed to be there and listened with the intent to understand instead of just waiting for their turn to talk? How different would your entire organization look if this were how meetings worked? This is completely achievable and a goal worth working towards. Let's change our organizations by changing something as innocuous as meetings.

Chapter 5
Correction or Development

CORRECTION AND DEVELOPMENT OF STAFF ARE DEMANDING. IT MEANS that you have held yourself accountable and know that you have provided every opportunity for a staff member to succeed. That is where the difference between development and correction comes into play. Your staff will all learn a process differently. Some will need a written manual that they read and can digest, others need to hear you explain it and watch you perform the tasks, and still, others will need to physically complete the task themselves before it will finally click. Development of staff is making sure you have covered each of these scenarios with all staff members.

Make sure that you, your young leaders, and your staff all understand that again, failure does not have to mean fear. We should not be leaders whose sole goal is to strike fear into the hearts of our staff. They should not be walking around on eggshells because they do not want to lose their jobs. There is a healthy amount of respect that everyone should carry for their position and organization to drive them to desire success. But in the words of Robert Downey Jr., "Everybody says, a Mistake is the first step of success. But the real fact is...correction of a Mistake is the first step of success." Take the time to correct mistakes with your staff and do not be a leader that just saves your staff. Your team will not learn to be successful if you are not allowing them the opportunity to learn from their own mistakes.

Walk through the why of the problem with your team. When they make a mistake take the time to walk them through the process and make sure they understand why what they did was a mistake and how to correct it moving forward. Make sure they are not sitting their mindlessly while you are talking watching a rerun of *Game of Thrones* in their head but that they are paying attention. Have them repeat it all back to you so you know they fully understand the workflow and the why.

As discussed previously, if someone can explain a process to you then they fully understand it. If they cannot explain it to you then they have not fully comprehended the entire process. Being able to tell whether they do not have the capacity to comprehend, the will to comprehend, or if we just need to try another tactic will fall to you. It is important to know that sometimes it is not one answer but a combination of tactics or responses. It is also important to realize that regardless of the scenario you must pay attention to the employee themselves. What personality type do they have? Have you provided all the tools that they need to be successful? Are they going through anything personally in their life that could be affecting their performance at work?

If there is another leader that they interact with, speak with that leader, and get some feedback on what they have noticed to be sure that you are not projecting or just seeing a small piece of the puzzle. It is crucial that you take the time to speak with that employee, there is often a misunderstanding or something else going on that you are not aware of. Beware of being a leader that makes snap judgments about people. Never assume you know the entire situation.

I had a supervisor who worked under me that I inherited from their previous leader. They were the best person at the job on the floor and had an incredible work ethic but had never been taught to lead. Because of this, she came across as very harsh or condescending sometimes to her team. My first reaction was to pull her aside and write her up for being so rude to the team. Turns out, her son was very sick, and she had spent the past few weeks up throughout the night taking care of him. She was also getting some attitude from the staff that they conveniently left out in their complaint of her.

My snap judgment reaction left her broken down in tears in my office and put me in a very difficult position. I had originally just judged that she must not be ready to be a leader and as I was young myself did not take that time upfront as I should have. Yet when I spoke with her more, I was able to meet her where she was and help her grow from there. When you take the time to meet your team or your young leader where they are then you can build a customized growth plan specific to that individual. You will also know quickly when something is off or if they are just the wrong fit for the role. Remember, just because someone is the best at the job does not mean that they are the best fit for leadership.

We are going to walk through a few scenarios, and I want you to keep this in mind. In the end, determine which option you feel is appropriate to handle the situation.

Scenario 1:

You have a new team leader who is responsible for onboarding and training the new staff. You have provided training tools and templates and taught them how you trained staff, so you are confident that they are capable of handling this task. However, after three weeks your new staff members are still struggling with their assignments, make multiple mistakes, and do not seem to be enjoying their days.

You decide to have a skip level one-on-one with your new staff members to see how they are doing but you ask your team lead first what their opinion is concerning the new team members. They reply that the new staff is difficult, have attitudes and are not teachable.

During your one-on-ones with the new staff, they state that the training is hard to understand, they feel like they have just been dropped in the deep end and they are not confident in their jobs. They also state that they feel your team lead is harsh and unrealistic in their expectations. You have only ever seen your team lead be encouraging and all the current staff love that team lead.

What are your next steps?
How would you solve this dilemma?

Option 1: Bring your team lead in and give them the feedback you received from the staff and ask why they have been so harsh. Proceed to remove training from that individual and take it back over until you feel like they are ready.

Option 2: Let the new staff know that the team leader is using approved documentation and training documents and that they need to focus more to ensure they understand the material. Tell them that the expectations for the job are challenging and if they cannot get with the program then maybe this is not the right place for them.

Option 3: Pull the team lead and the new staff members into a training room for a refresher, meet with the team lead beforehand to provide some ideas on how else they could reach their new staff members, and coach them on making sure they are paying attention to their tone and being careful of their word usage. Then observe and step in as needed to make the training dynamic and interactive.

Which option do you feel was the best response and assisted both the young leader and the staff to get what they needed to be successful?

Scenario 2:

You have a staff member on the floor that you have spent the past 4 months attempting to get on the right path. You have spent dedicated one-on-one time with them, trained them in various ways, including using others to train, and you have had multiple developmental conversations with this employee. One afternoon you are walking through the floor, and you hear a raised voice. You look over and that employee is shouting into the phone at a client using unprofessional language and then slams the phone down.

How do you handle this scenario?

Option 1: You yell across the floor, "What do you think you are doing?! Get your things and get out!" After this, you proceed immediately to the HR office to let them know you have immediately fired an employee for inappropriate language and verbal abuse of a client.

Option 2: Make a mental note to talk to this employee about their behavior in their next one-on-one. They are more than likely just having a bad day and need some time to cool off.

Option 3: Quietly walk over to the employee's desk and ask them to take a few minutes to get back under control and then please meet you in your office in 10 minutes. During those

10 minutes, inform HR that we are going to be having a tough conversation and go ahead and write up a final in case it is needed depending on the staff response, so you are prepared.

When the staff member comes into your office you shut the door and ask them what is going on. You have noticed that their performance over the past few months has not been up to the standards you know they are capable of and the actions on the floor today were out of line. The staff member rolls their eyes and crosses their arms and states that they are just going through a hard time right now and they are sorry.

You go ahead and inform them that due to the severity of the behavior on the floor you are going to give them a final written warning. They have two weeks to show improvement and correct the behavior. If they do not show improvement or correction, then it could possibly lead to termination. You ask if they need any further support and offer to have someone in HR reach out for any personal assistance. You also provide them with the phone number of the company that your organization uses to counsel staff.

After showing them the final written you give them 15 minutes to compose themselves before going back out onto the floor.

Which option seems like it will have the best ending?

SCENARIO 3:

You have a manager under you that is responsible for two teams. They have a supervisor and team lead for each of those teams and you noticed that you have seen those supervisors working overtime on a consistent basis. When you speak to the supervisors, they seem nervous and agitated and state that they are working very hard and not to worry that they will complete all their work. The next day you speak with their manager and ask what tasks are requiring the supervisors to work so much overtime and they provide a vague answer and hint that the supervisors are not very good at time management.

HOW DO YOU HANDLE THIS SITUATION?

Option 1: You coach that manager on how to assist their supervisors with time management and then watch the situation closely to see if the overtime improves as well as the nervousness of the supervisors.

Option 2: You go directly to the supervisors and talk to them about time management skills and encourage them to limit their overtime.

Option 3: You obtain more information regarding the work the supervisors are performing and then work with that manager to reallocate responsibilities so that the manager can assist the supervisors until they are more comfortable with their responsibilities.

This one is tricky. You could technically do any of these options or even a combination of them. Which option do you feel would be the most beneficial for your whole team and for the growth of both sets of leaders?

Scenario 4:

You have a new supervisor who was the absolute best at the job when they were on the floor. They were the trainer and who everyone went to with their questions. Due to this, they were made supervisors. After a few months, you notice that the productivity and the attitude of the team seem to be going down. You have been having weekly one-on-ones with the supervisor and spent weeks training them and coaching them on their role and responsibilities as well as how to lead their staff.

Even after this time, the supervisor seems overly stressed out and the team seems to be picking up on and responding to that feeling. What are your next steps?

Option 1: This is a loyal and great employee so you continue to just try and give them encouragement that they can do this!

Option 2: You see that they clearly are not capable of handling a leadership position, so you demote them to their previous position.

Option 3: During your next one-on-one you discuss the supervisor's take on leadership and whether it was what they thought it was going to be. You discuss other opportunities in the organization that would allow them to move into a new role but not requires them to lead staff.

Which scenario seems like the best fit?

At times in my career, I have encountered each of these scenarios and more. You must decide, and often quickly if you are going to take the time to develop that individual, or if you are going to just move straight to corrective action. Sometimes, the answer is a little of both. I want to give you a few examples of some nightmare corrective action moments that I have experienced. I had a staff member who had a constant attitude with her Manager, Supervisor, and other department's teams. We had received multiple complaints about her behavior and had spent a few months attempting to work with her on emotional intelligence and being able to hear herself when she spoke to other people.

She was already on a first written warning for her behavior when I received a phone call that she had walked over to another department and began discussing a staff member's quality score with a different employee. Not only were they doing this, but they were also doing this on the call center floor, next to that staff member's desk, while he was on the phone with a member! As you can imagine this created quite a bit of anger and frustration in that staff member as well as anger on the other department leader I was speaking to. After discussing the situation with HR and her manager we decided to place her on a final written warning due to the severity of her behavior.

At this time, we pulled her into my office, had her manager and HR in the room with us, and walked through the reason she was being placed on a final written warning. At that moment, she became extremely combative and aggressive in her word choices and body language. At one point in the conversation, she even began to lean over my desk in an attempt to intimidate me and assert herself. Now, before I move forward, take a moment and picture yourself in that scenario, how would you have responded?

HR was ready to terminate her on the spot for insubordination, and while I did consider it, I also knew how hard she worked, and the attitude was the only issue. So, I took one last shot with this employee. I decided that if she responded well, we would keep her on the final and move forward, if she continued down this aggressive path then we would walk her out the door. Very calmly I asked her to take a step back from my desk and sit back down. I assured her that she was not being attacked but that her behavior was in no way acceptable and would not be tolerated. Never raising my voice, but leaning forward on my desk a little, I stated that if she wanted to remain employed then we would love to work with her on adjusting her behavior and attitude. However, I am also willing to accept resignations if she did not feel that this was the right position for her.

Before the extremely intense meeting was over, we agreed to keep her on a final with a 30-day expectation. Within 30 days we expected to see vastly improved performance and we expected to see an immediate difference in her attitude and behavior. We would be having weekly one-on-one with her manager and they would be discussing emotional intelligence and customer experience. Three months later she was still with the organization, had never created another disturbance, and was a very high-performing employee.

Now, I am positive I could have handled some of that conversation a little better. Leaning forward on my desk was a reaction on my part that I had to learn from. Not only was I dealing with an employee, but I also had a manager that I was mentoring in the room watching my response to such an aggressive employee. There will be many people with many different opinions on how I should have handled that situation and I appreciate the fact that different personalities respond differently. However, the most important takeaway is to remember to respond and not react. When we react, we escalate the situation further and we create a hostile environment that we are participating in. This will never create a healthy culture and will often exacerbate whatever situation you are in.

Create an environment where, even when you have an aggressive reaction from a staff member during a corrective action conversation, your response remains professional, calm, and measured. While their reaction may very well take them past that final warning to immediate termination, you need to be sure that you are not pushing that staff member into a greater frenzy with your reaction. You are responsible for your responses, regardless of the situation, the leader in the room should always be the example of how to handle a situation. Even if that means you must take ten seconds and breathe before responding. As long as you are not counting down from ten out loud, it can absolutely help dissolve some tension in the room.

The last example I will leave you with is providing a written warning to a staff member that I had spent the past 3 months training, retraining, coaching, and providing guidance to. They had a great personality but did not seem to be grasping the position. They continued to make the same mistakes repeatedly, so I decided to place them on a first written warning. They had already had coaching conversations and a verbal so the first written was the next appropriate step.

I pulled up the first written warning document and prefilled it with specific dates, examples, and screenshots of what we would be discussing and then scheduled a meeting with that employee. At this organization all staff, including myself, were remote so this conversation happened over a team's meeting. During the call, I began the conversation by letting them know that unfortunately, we are here to discuss some ongoing issues we have seen with their performance. As we have provided multiple pieces of training and have already had a verbal conversation with the expectations clearly laid out, we would be enforcing a first written warning today.

The next step was to pull up the form and share my screen so we can walk through the scenarios together. We walked through each situation, and I had the employee walk me through how they felt they could have performed differently and how they can make adjustments moving forward. At the end of the conversation, I thanked them for their time and informed them that I expected these corrections to take immediate effect and that they had two weeks to apply the tools we had discussed today. At the end of the two weeks, we will have a follow-up discussion and if improvements are not made, we will need to move to the next step in the corrective action process. They thanked me for the opportunity and assured me that they would make those corrections moving forward and understood why they were being written up that day.

My principal rule when performing corrective action or terminations is that the employee should never be surprised by the conversation. This means that you have taken the time to provide coaching opportunities, extra training, verbal and written communications, laid out the expectations, and had them relay them back to you so you know they understand. Once you have performed all these functions and you bring someone in for a written warning it should not come as a surprise. Be detailed and have examples of the reason for the corrective action and provide abundantly clear expectations for that person

Corrective Action Notice
Date of Incident:

Employee Name:

Position:

Department:

TYPE OF VIOLATION

ATTENDANCE (UNEXCUSED)		CARELESSNESS / SAFETY		INSUBORDINATION / CONDUCT	
OTHER POLICY VIOLATION		JOB PERFORMANCE		POOR CUSTOMER SERVICE	

THIS VIOLATION HAS RESULTED IN THE FOLLOWING CORRECTIVE ACTION

LEVEL OF ACTION	DATE	BY WHOM	COMMENTS
VERBAL / COUNSELING (Manager's Documentation)			
WRITTEN WARNING			
TERMINATION			

Should your performance and/or conduct become unsatisfactory again or continue to be unsatisfactory based on the above or any other company policy, rule or regulation, this may result in further disciplinary action, up to and including termination, for any other occurrence of any problem.

EMPLOYER STATEMENT:

HANDBOOK VIOLATION:

_____ I concur with Employer's statement.   _____ I disagree with Employer's description of the violation. The reasons are:

_____

_____

Signature: _____   Date: _____

I have read this Employee Warning Notice and understand it.

Employee Signature	Print Name	Date

moving forward as well as a timeframe on when you will be following up with them again.

If you do ever have the unfortunate experience of terminating an employee, it is important to remember a few things. Remember to deal in facts and not feelings and keep the conversation short and simple. HR should always be involved in that conversation so they can provide the employee with their next steps, how to return any equipment and when their last paycheck will be sent to them. Your part of the conversation should go something like this:

"Thank you for meeting with us today. Unfortunately, we have determined that due to your performance over the past few months we have decided that this is not the right fit for you, and we are going to be terminating your employment effective immediately. We understand that this is not an easy time, so I am going to have Joe from HR walk you through the next steps." Then stop, if the employee attempts to ask questions or keep the conversation going do not argue or engage. Allow your HR team to handle the conversation from there.

Remember, you are impacting someone's life. You are impacting their children and family's lives. This should be taken seriously and should not be a decision you make as a knee-jerk reaction or on a whim because you are angry. Make this decision with a cool head and the counsel of your HR department. Always make sure you have documented every conversation, corrective action, coaching, and one-on-one for reference as needed. If you did not write it down, it did not happen. Therefore, it is important to have written policies and procedures, written follow-up emails from your one-on-one meetings and huddles, and documented coaching, training, and corrective action conversations. Make sure you are listening to your staff and not just going through the motions.

One issue that will be different depending on the policies at your organization is announcing departures. A problem I have repeatedly run into is that individuals would resign, get fired, or be included in a reduction in force, and yet the leadership would not inform anyone else in the organization. Therefore, people would continue to send teams messages or emails to that individual and wonder why they did not send a response. Eventually, they would start receiving an email back stating the email was invalid and would come to ask questions. This always bothered me, and I believe there is a better way to handle it. When there is a member of your team that leaves, regardless of the reason, the individuals who worked with that person have a right to know so that we are not impeding their ongoing work. They do not need the details, and in fact, have no right to the details, however, they do need to know who to contact moving forward.

With this in mind, I want to discuss one more piece of this development and correction puzzle that is also quite challenging. Discretion. Your friends, coworkers, staff members, or even other leaders do not have the right to know all the details surrounding an employee's departure. If you are going to be letting someone go, do not go discuss this with anyone else on that team, other leaders, or anyone outside of HR and your direct supervisor. Regardless of how much you feel as if you trust someone, believe they will not say anything, or think it is no big deal, it will often come back to bite you. I have seen other leaders warn staff members that they were fixing to get fired and that staff members then vindictively created problems by deleting files, destroying systems, or stealing information off their computers. I have seen rumors spread like wildfire and before you can blink you have lost the trust of your entire team over a rumor that is perhaps not even true.

Even after someone is no longer with the organization, do not negatively discuss that individual with anyone in the organization aside from HR or possibly your own supervisor if you run into issues that need to be resolved. Think about it from a personal perspective, how many friends or acquaintances do you know that get really excited to be the one who knows? How many stories do you hear a day or week concerning others in your organization and who is telling those stories? Do you remember the game telephone as a child? Everyone would stand in a line, and someone would whisper a word or phrase into the next person's ear. This would continue down the line until the message had been passed all the way down the line. The last person then says, out loud, what they think the message was. We, of course, would giggle and laugh whenever the phrase was completely unrecognizable from the original phrase.

This does not stop as we get older. Whether intentionally or not, the message gets changed. With this in mind, be careful who you are talking to regarding staff. You should not have to walk around your offices paranoid and spend all day peeking through your office blinds wondering who is going to

First One-on-One Meeting

Team Member Name:	Date:
Title/ Position:	Time:

Greeting / Personal Connection (5 mins)

(How is life? Have you tried anything fun lately?)

Notes:

Overview (5 mins)

Briefly go over the agenda and meeting guidelines
- What the employee can expect from one-on-ones
- Open and honest communication
- How often one-on-ones should occur

Issues & Feedback (10 mins)

Any interesting observations so far?

Have you run into any challenges or roadblocks?

What would you like further training or clarification on?

Goals (5 mins)

What are your goals going forward? (Long-term career goals?)

1.
2.

betray whom next, but you should pay attention and exercise discretion when discussing the disciplinary actions of an employee with anyone else.

Most importantly remember this, just like everything else in leadership, corrective action and development take work. At the end of the day, correction should not be a snap judgment or something that is taken lightly. Ruling your office by fear is not a way to build a healthy and fully functional team. "Correction does much, but encouragement does more." John Wolfgang Von Goethe.

Chapter 6
Culture Shock

Now that we have discussed some of the harder aspects of leadership let's discuss something that can be quite a bit of fun. Creating a company culture that is healthy and vibrant is just as important as creating operational processes and standard operating procedures. A company's culture is the lifeblood of an organization. If you have a healthy culture your organization will thrive, if you have an unhealthy culture, it is like having cancer in your bloodstream. It will make your organization sick, and you will struggle to thrive. A toxic environment results in high turnover rates, nervous and uncomfortable staff that are not willing to put their whole selves into their work, and a group of people who work for a paycheck instead of for passion.

Every organization I have ever worked with has struggled with culture. This is always due to the leadership team. It has always seemed odd to me that leaders are happy to strut around an office with their chest puffed out to show they are in charge, but when it comes to taking ownership for things such as culture, development, accountability, and quality they are very quick to turn and point at the staff, other leadership or even the political or national climate. When you have a leader who displays a culture of excuses and finger-pointing, what do you think their staff will look like?

Taking accountability is the beginning of creating a positive and effective culture. In the movie *Remember the Titans* two players are arguing about each other's behavior on the field. The team captain points out that the other individual has the worst attitude he has ever heard. The response he received back changed his thought process. His team member looked him right in the eye

47

and said, "Attitude reflects leadership, Captain." When you have a leadership team that takes ownership of their organization's culture watch out! There is nothing that a team cannot accomplish if they are all rowing in the same direction. Just like the Titans, this process of creating a positive culture does not always have to take years to accomplish either. If you have an organization with an extremely unhealthy culture now, it is fixable. Sometimes this does, unfortunately, mean that not everyone currently with your team stays with your team, but that is entirely up to them.

Culture is implementing everything we have talked about so far and everything else we will talk about. Accountability, building leaders that build leaders, appropriate development, and corrective action, showing your team how to handle failure, and mentoring new staff and young leaders. All of these build the foundations of a company culture that will live on well past your department or even your tenure in the organization.

Recently I joined an organization that had a confused culture. This organization has been around for many years and had multiple individuals in my seat before me, each bringing their flavor and processes to the team. Unfortunately, much of that ended up being something that was taught to new staff but was never taken back to current staff and implemented, which resulted in a confused and argumentative team.

The first step I took was clearing the air. I pulled each of my teams together and just gave them one rule. We will always speak to, write, and treat everyone with kindness and respect. This includes your coworkers, insurance companies, vendors, clients, and other departments in this organization. If we can start there, if we can begin to treat each other with the respect that every individual deserves, we can work out the rest. This is easier said than done and we had many opportunities to remind the staff to speak with respect. During this time, we began taking processes one at a time and breaking them down.

I used my first month of one-on-ones with all my staff to gain their perspective on all the processes, job responsibilities, and the flow of their day along with their expectations on what was reasonable to ask for them to accomplish daily. After documenting all this information, I met with my COO and we discussed which processes made sense, which we were going to slightly tweak, and which we were going to throw out and replace altogether. This must be strategically done as you cannot expect your team to learn an entirely new workflow and expectations overnight, but you also do not want this transformation to take years. We identified the areas that needed the most immediate correction and began there.

Unsurprisingly, this was the expectation of the positions. To accomplish this we rewrote job descriptions, updated manuals, and corrected SOPs as needed to support their new expectations. We provided updated training for the entire staff together so we could be sure everyone was on the same page, and I met with everyone on a weekly or biweekly basis to check in with their status and also how they were receiving the changes. An important thing to remember, that most leaders do not, is that you are not the person on the floor performing that job. Whatever expectations, policies and procedures, and rules you enforce on your staff must make sense to them. If you implement an entirely unrealistic expectation, as we discussed in a previous chapter, then you have set your team up to fail before they begin, and you will watch your culture go down instead of up.

When you take the time to include the team in the building of their processes then they take ownership of them. This does not mean letting them create low expectations or lowering the standards you have for your team. It means showing them the why and the how of their position. When everyone in the company feels as if they have ownership in their role and the team then they take pride in it that cannot be achieved by simply being told what to do. They are more likely to begin challenging themselves and those around them to reach a higher goal or see how much more they can accomplish when they see what their work means. If you are sitting in a corner, or at home by yourself, just inputting data into a screen, or sitting on the phone all day it can become very monotonous, depressing, and boring. Your staff begins to believe that what they do does not matter that much so they begin to slow down, lower their expectations, and check out mentally during the day.

My current teams work very hard to get our patients in the door for a treatment that can save their lives. When you are sitting on hold with United Healthcare or are continually getting the runaround from Cigna it can be hard to remember that. For this reason, we share great news at the beginning of our meetings, and we also have a Teams group for the whole organization where the clinical directors share amazing testimonies from our patients. This lets the administrative teams see what they helped accomplish by sitting on hold and getting that patient approved for treatment. As John Welch states, "No company, small or large, can win over the long run without energized employees who believe in the mission and understand how to achieve it."

Be a company that celebrates the wins with your teams and not just points out the failures or the pieces that need changing. Encourage some interoffice communication between your teams when appropriate to encourage a healthy team who learns to work together. Create a culture of learning and development where your team gets excited to learn new processes and see improvements. You do this by sharing the why behind the changes and showing them the results of their efforts. Who doesn't like to see how their hard work has paid off?

During a one-on-one with my youngest and newest leader, she mentioned that before we began this new process of culture correction that she was having to drag herself out of bed every day and was looking for another position. Now, however, she had stopped looking for another position and was leaning into the changes. She started seeing the change happen in all the clinics she worked with, the leadership was more approachable, she was less afraid of making a mistake, and felt like she could bring me any problem knowing that I would help her find a solution. By taking the time weekly to create a calm and learning environment she felt that I freely shared my wisdom, provided direction and feedback instead of criticism and silence and she understood the why now. By taking the time to teach her how to accomplish the expectations that had been given to her, she had a newfound confidence and woke up excited to come into work today. The other leaders and staff around her have noted a new passion and energy in her daily interactions and she is proud to work for us now.

It took everything I had to follow my own rules and not let her see the tears in my eyes. This is my why. This is the reward for wringing myself out every day and logging off mentally exhausted at the end of the day. Knowing that I have helped not only change her perspective and life but now everything she is learning will reach more people than I ever could on my own. This is how you grow company culture. By taking the time to spend with your leadership teams, getting everyone on board, rowing in the same direction, and showing your team a united and positive front. When you feel that your leadership team is cool, calm, and collected then you have more peace and confidence in your position.

When we take the time to step outside of ourselves and look at the world from our staff's perspective and show them that we are listening, paying attention, and are doing something about their concerns, you win over a staff that wants to get up and come to work every day. Let's go back to *Remember the Titans*, for those of you who have not seen the movie, you need to! Talk about a culture shock! After receiving feedback from his teammate about attitude reflecting leadership the young man thought this through and decided to make a change. Once he started holding everyone accountable to the same standards, starting with himself, and once he started making a concerted effort to build a relationship with his teammates, regardless of the color of their skin, the entire atmosphere changed. His teacher took their cue from him and they came home a changed team that was willing to fight for each other in an environment that fought them at every turn. He even decided on his own to cut his best friend because he knew that he was hurting the team around him. Not only did he do that, but he took ownership of the decision and informed that teammate that he was out because of his behavior. Talk about accountability.

While letting someone go does not seem to jive with creating a positive culture remember what Gary says in *Remember the Titans:* "Sometimes you have to cut a man loose." If you have individuals on your team that is poisoning the positive culture you are trying to build and have been allowed to get on board but only continue to hurt those around them, maybe it is time to cut them loose. In healthcare, you must cut away the infection or it will continue to grow and damage the body. To create a whole and healthy organization you have to have the right person, right seat mentality for the good of the organization. Even if that means that your best friend is not the right person.

In the world we are in, depending on your organization, sometimes it feels as if you are fighting an uphill battle at every turn. But when your team sees that you are fighting for them and working to create a more positive and productive environment, inclusive of holding yourself and your team accountable to the laid-out expectations then you end up with a team that will fight for each other and you.

By taking the time upfront you create a culture that assists you in moving forward so everything does not end up falling on your shoulders. You do not have to carry the entire company around on your back when you create the right culture. You can even take a vacation and not have to look at your phone the entire time because you can trust that your team has it covered while you are resting on a beach somewhere, recharging your batteries.

So, take the time, hold yourself and your team accountable, make sure you have the right person in the right seat, create a positive learning environment, and take your staff's thoughts into account when creating their expectations and responsibilities as well as their processes and procedures. You will not believe how quickly you can turn an organization around by focusing on the culture instead of focusing on the money or production.

Chapter 7
How to Handle Failure

WE HAVE BRIEFLY TOUCHED ON HANDLING FAILURE THROUGH THE ENTIRE book, so why are we dedicating another entire chapter to it? Because this will determine whether your organization and leaders fail or if they succeed in the long run. Failure is such a scary word. From childhood, we do not like to fail. I have seen kids bring home an A- in the 3rd grade and be hysterical about the thought that they did not receive perfect marks. Of course, not every child is like this, but even if it is not grades, everyone is afraid of failing at something. The most confident person you know has a fear of failure on some level. So, if we know that our staff, leaders, and teams all have a fear of failure, and we are working to create a culture of positivity, learning, growth, and healthy communication, then how do we handle the fear aspect?

I have mentored so many leaders that all had the same problem, fearing that they would fail me, themselves, and their staff. They so desperately wanted to be taken seriously and prove that they could handle their role that they often took things upon themselves that they could not handle. I would have leaders that would leave and go home and work another five or six hours every night for months trying to solve a problem before I could catch wind of it. I have seen staff members go to extreme lengths to hide their mistakes to prevent their leadership from knowing that they failed for fear of the repercussions. Let me tell you the same thing I tell my four-year-old: When you lie and hide things you get into more trouble than if you would have admitted to what you did wrong.

When you try and hide that spilled milk on the couch by just throwing a blanket on top of it then I might not notice it that day, but eventually, I am going to move that blanket, my couch is going to be ruined and smell horrible and I am going to have a much harder time cleaning that and fixing the problem. Getting staff to understand the same concept is just as difficult as it is with my kids. When we hide problems for fear of failure then we create a bigger problem that might not be as fixable.

I was guilty of this myself in my first leadership position. I wanted to prove that I had earned that position and did not want my leader having any doubt that I could handle anything that came my way. When they would ask me how everything was going my answers were always positive: "Things are great!" "Going well." Or my personal favorite, "Oh, yes, I am fine." Little did I know, my leader was sitting there thinking, oh really? They were waiting on me to come to ask for help because they knew that although I was good, there was no way I was that good. And they were right. My error in not seeking out help or advice when I needed it for fear of failing or even appearing to have failed led to an extremely stressful six months of my life, a neurotic and unhealthy culture for my team, and missed opportunities for my organization.

When I finally came to my leader I was in tears and apologizing for my mistakes. At that point, because I had waited so long, there were some things they could fix, and others they could not. I was extremely lucky to be given another chance and to keep my job. That leader took the time, once they knew I would listen, and walked me through how to go about fixing the errors I had inadvertently created. They did not fix them for me, I had to work hard to fix them myself, but they stood next to me during every step and guided my feet to prevent another misstep on my part.

While I learned there were consequences for my actions, I also learned how to accept help and that failure does not have to mean fear. My boss laid it out to me like this, in our industry most of what we did was fixable and not life-threatening. There are roles, of course, where failure means the life of that person on the operating table or an accident that gets your fellow soldiers killed. Those are horrible consequences to failures that are not fixable and are not quite as easy to move on from. However, how many of those errors were caused because the people were fearful of failure and refused to seek counsel or help?

Now, just because failure does not have to mean fear it also does not mean that we brush it off as no big deal and take a cavalier attitude towards the quality of our work. It means that we overcome that fear of failure and reach out for help as we need it. Get that clarification on the project specifications, ask for more training or a refresher on the sales pitch or let your leader know that no you are not okay, and you have had a rough week and could use some advice on how to handle a tough situation. This is tricky from both sides of the desk. The leader asking for help is putting themselves in a vulnerable position and the leader on the other side of the desk needs to remember that. Remember the fear you had when you were in their position and then take the knowledge and wisdom you have fought hard to learn and help pass that on to the next in line. It does no good whatsoever to belittle or judge your team members if you are not willing to get down in the muck and mire with them to find a solution. As John Quincy Adams said, "If your actions inspire others to dream more, learn more, do more, and become more, you are a leader." Do your actions inspire your teams and leaders, or do they instill more fear in them?

When you think back over your career and life who most inspired you? What characteristics did they display? Who were your favorite teachers in school? After all, teachers are just leaders of our youth. My favorite teachers were the ones that jumpstarted my imagination. They encouraged creativity and thinking outside of the box. They did not make me conform or fit into a test but taught me things that mattered to me and made me interested to learn more. They knew that if they could teach me concepts and if they could get me to love or at least understand their subject, passing the test become automatic. Whenever we failed at something they would take that opportunity to step down to my level, meet me where I was and help guide me out.

As leaders that is part of our job. This is one of those touchy subjects that leaders do not always agree with, and that is okay. However, ask yourself what it costs you, in the long run, to not take the time with your team. When we practice what we preach and get down on the level of our team and help them understand how to admit to and learn from failure then we build a team that can achieve anything. By admitting our failure, not placing blame on others, or creating a dozen excuses, then we can begin to handle failure.

The next steps are just as crucial. Once you have admitted and acknowledged your failure, then start thinking of a way to fix it. If you are a leader who is always looking for someone else to fix your mistakes or have staff that constantly make an error, but you bail them out all of the time, then you are not learning from it. Failure is only helpful when we learn. Otherwise, it is just failure. Stepping down and helping your staff see the way out does not mean you pick up their failure and carrying it on your shoulders and leaving them to just casually walk right out, they do not learn that way. Let them carry their failure and guide them out, if they need a supporting hand, of course, lend that to them. Help them by showing them the way, helping them get their mind in the right place, and being a sounding board for them on how to fix an issue.

I had a Vice President I reported up through who was so good at this it was almost annoying. I would come into his office and let him know that someone on my team or myself had made a mistake and I was not sure what to do about it. He would sit back in his chair and ask what I had already tried. If I did not have an answer or had not tried, he would smile at me, and I would know that I needed to go make my effort and stop taking the easy way out. He knew that I would never learn if he saved me all the time. He would usually point me in the right direction or give me a nudge towards an idea to try but he did expect me to go handle it on my own. After going out and trying to think it through I could almost always come to a solution on my own. At this point, I would bound back into his office excited at my success! I was just sure he was going to pat me on the back and celebrate my brilliant problem-solving skills.

What happened, he would listen patiently to my explanation of what path I chose to correct the issue and then he would ask me one or two questions: "What made you take that route?" or "Why was that the path you took?" This question would always unnerve me because that old fear of failure would kick in. However, I knew I was in a safe space so I would walk him through the steps and how I came to the conclusion I did. Often he would say, "Sounds great, keep me posted if you need anything else." But occasionally he would nod his head and then say, "What about...," and would walk me through another scenario that did not even come to mind. This would get my mind churning again and created opportunities for me to learn from not only my own mistakes but my team's failures as well.

He understood that failure is going to happen and my response to that failure was as important as the identification of the failure itself. By allowing me to come to my conclusions he was not saving me from my failure or my team's. Instead, he was making me save myself and think through solutions, get creative and work with my team to discover a solution that we would remember the next time, or better yet that would prevent the mistake again in the future. After all, the whole point of learning from our failure is to learn how to prevent that failure moving forward. Picking ourselves up, brushing off the dust, and having the courage to step forward will separate our organizations from everyone else.

Theodore Roosevelt could not have said it better in his man in the arena speech:

> "It is not the critic who counts; not the man who points out how the strong man stumbles, or where the doer of deeds could have done them better. The credit belongs to the man who is actually in the arena, whose face is marred by dust and sweat and blood; who strives valiantly; who errs, who comes short again and again, because there is no effort without error and shortcoming; but who does strive to do the deeds; who knows great enthusiasms, the great devotions; who spends himself in a worthy cause; who at the best knows, in the end, the triumph of high achievement, and who at the worst, if he fails, at least fails while daring greatly, so that his place shall never be with those cold and timid souls who neither know victory nor defeat."

Basically, there is no success, no learning, no growth, and no movement when we live our lives and teach our staff to be afraid of failure. Albert Einstein even said that "Failure is success in progress." He is 100% right. Do you think that any major company got to where they are because they made all the right decisions? More importantly, did you get to your leadership position without making some missteps?

If we create a culture of learning, then we create an environment where failure is an opportunity to grow instead of an excuse to correct. The difference between a good leader and a bad or even mediocre leader is their ability to take ownership and learn from failure, not letting it weigh them or their team down but taking that failure and turning it into a steppingstone for greatness.

Chapter 8
Build Something to Outlive You

WHEN WE TEACH ALL THESE SKILLS TO THE LEADERS COMING BEHIND US then we build a lasting impression that will outlive our time with that organization. When we take the stance that everyone should have to come to us for everything because we are the boss then we are robbing those that report to us from learning, growing, and experiencing any success on their own. This is a trend that is extremely prevalent in leadership and one that should be eradicated immediately. An insecure leader tends to withhold knowledge, information, and growth opportunities from their team due to a fear that they will be challenged, questioned or even have their leadership overthrown.

If we are afraid of our team taking our job, then we should step outside of ourselves and think about whether we could be doing more to earn the position we are in. If we are the only person who knows how to perform a function or who can make a decision because you are the only one who knows all the pieces, then you think they have job security. We discussed this earlier as well and I want to reiterate it here. When you feel like withholding information is the only way you can keep your job then you are a poor excuse for a leader that is hurting not only yourself but your team and your organization.

I have mentored and counseled many leaders who come in angry and bitter or exhausted and worn out because they feel that they never get a break, and the company is always taking advantage of them. They never get to take a vacation and no one else understands how hard their job is. My first two questions are always the same. Have you written all your processes down? And who have you begun training to do what you do? Without fail, I receive a look of shock that I would even suggest such a thing. Being a leader does not mean we are incapable of creating our own self-importance to an unhealthy and damaging level. Sometimes it even seems to drive people to that point.

The desperate attempt to prove our value and worth leads people to think that they cannot possibly let anyone else know what they do, or they will become replaceable and obsolete. Let me share something that I had to learn too; everyone is replaceable. This is not intended to strike fear or discomfort into your hearts and minds. When we have a healthy mindset as a leader this should be a freeing and still challenging sentiment. It should create in us the desire to prove ourselves by showing our growth potential. If we are not going to teach someone else how to think like we do or perform a task and if we are unwilling to be challenged, then we will only ever accomplish what we can accomplish alone.

When we are willing to be challenged by others and teach those around us our knowledge then we increase our influence and reach across our team and our whole organization. It becomes a comfort to know that we are allowed a sick day or a vacation because we can trust that our team has got it covered. Our pride can come from the actions of our team and watching everyone become more successful instead of our pride coming from only what we can accomplish on our own. As we allow others into our mind and knowledge it is a vulnerable and scary thing because all of the sudden you have someone "beneath" you are asking you why. I have had fellow leaders come storming into my office and slam the door furious that their staff would question their instructions. After all, they were the boss, they were the leader, and the staff should just do as they are told. I would usually ask the situation and would try to contain my smile as they would begin describing how they finally decided to teach someone how to do something and they dared suggest or ask if they could do it a different way.

They would snort in derision and begin complaining about that staff member being, as we say in the south, too big for their britches. I would casually ask what their suggestion was and, if they could even remember, they would tell me. Regardless of if it was a good or bad suggestion, I would say that is great! To which I would receive a confusing and wary look. If your team is thinking and trying to come up with solutions that means they are engaged! That is a success. Maybe let them try some of their suggestions and see where it takes them. Who knows, maybe you will discover a more efficient way to do a process. Sometimes the leader would see how silly they were acting and would calm down and let their team try and often the leader would refuse any suggestions and would have a litany of excuses why they probably would not work.

Being open to change from those around you, especially those you are teaching, is a challenge that many leaders struggle with daily. Learning from someone that you should be training and developing is humbling. Well, maybe we could use a little humbling. If you allow those you are mentoring, teaching, leading, and training to think for themselves and get creative then they are going to be more ready for leadership when it is their turn. Leaders have to think quickly on their feet and come up with out-of-the-box solutions sometimes. If you are stunting the growth of the leaders or staff underneath you by taking that option away from them then they are going to have a much harder time as a leader themselves.

But, if you teach them how to be creative, help them problem solve, and encourage them to continuously improve processes, even if that means changing your process, then they will be ready to step into that role. You will have built something that outlives you. Your influence and guidance will be remembered even after you move up or move out of that position. Think about it this way, you are going to be remembered one way or another, you control how you will be remembered through your actions. If you are difficult, refuse to teach or let anyone else in on your thought process, or refuse to change a process out of stubbornness then you will be remembered with an eye roll and a shudder. If you encourage your teams and your leaders to learn, grow, think outside the box and are open to changing yourself then you will be remembered and referenced fondly.

Leadership itself becomes easier because you are constantly growing those around you and letting them grow those around them so before you know it you can look around and see your influence on staff members you have never even spoken to or over departments that do not report to you. You gain new opportunities to keep growing and learning yourself or, if it is that time, you can retire knowing that you left the organization better than when you found it.

After all, who wants to walk away from something that you have invested your energy, time away from your family, mind, and heart into knowing that it is going to fail because no one else can do what you do? No! If you are a healthy individual and a good leader, you want to retire knowing that you can rest in peace not worrying about how your team is doing and how they are handling the projects that started as your baby. You want to know that you have spent your career building a legacy that will live on past you and can look back with pride knowing that you helped start something that will keep growing and live on.

Chapter 9
Transition Plans

THIS LEADS ME TO OUR NEXT TOPIC: TRANSITION PLANS. WHETHER YOU are transitioning into a new role, retirement, or a new company, you need to make sure you have a clean and well-thought-out transition plan for the person who will have to step into your hard-to-fill shoes. The same thing is true when you have staff underneath you who are transitioning out of their roles or a new staff member transitioning into a role. People hear transition plans and think it means the end of something. Sometimes this is true, but it also means the beginning of something else.

For example, we are in a hyper-growth mode at my organization, which means that the leaders are all wearing multiple hats while we search for the right person to put in the right seat. As we are opening new clinics our current clinical directors are traveling to those locations, taking telehealth visits, and working extra time to get that new clinic up and running. As we bring on a new clinical director to take over that clinic, we have a transition plan for the clinical director covering to transition the clinic over to the new and permanent clinical director. This is something to celebrate and not something to have anxiety over.

Transition plans should be well-laid-out documents including how-to training, SOPs, rules and regulations, onboarding documents, and clear job expectations and descriptions. There should be a specific time laid out for the person transitioning in and out that details what should be discussed on what day so that you can be sure everything is transitioned and the person coming into a role is not left with only half the information. Making sure that they have access to all systems, folders, permissions, and locations in your organization that are necessary for their position is also vital.

If we had a new clinical director and trained them on everything but then left with the keys, that does not exactly set us up for success. The same would be true if we trained them how to open but did not train them what was necessary to close or appropriately care for the equipment in the clinic. This can lead to disaster if you come back to check a couple of months later and realize that the equipment has not been maintained appropriately.

Just like everything else we have discussed, this falls on leadership. It does not fall on the person coming into the role and it might not even fall on the person leaving a role. After all, you should not have anyone in your organization who is the only person who knows their job, right? Right! So glad we are on the same page. As the leader over this position, it is your responsibility to make sure that the person transitioning out has a red-carpet experience and the person transitioning in has a red-carpet experience.

There are, of course, many ways of doing this. Have the current leader put together a training notebook documenting any nuances that are not already written down and pull all the training and SOP documents together for them. Or you could create a One Drive folder that has all the necessary documentation in it so that it can be updated without having to throw away any physical documents. You can have the person transitioning out train the incoming staff member or leader, or you can train them yourself or even have the training department train them if you have an individual department.

Truthfully you should always make sure that you are spending dedicated and extra time with your new leaders and staff to ensure that you can build that report and begin to build trust as early as possible. As we have already concluded, leadership is responsible for creating company culture so being sure to spend the necessary time with those transitioning in so they understand and are comfortable is essential to maintaining your culture.

If you have a current staff member who is simply transitioning into a new role then you need to make sure their previous role is sufficiently trained on and transitioned as well as their new role is sufficiently trained on and transitioned. This will mean that that individual goes through two separate transitions, sometimes simultaneously. Make sure that they understand they are not alone in their transition and that they are supported throughout. Be available to them as they have questions but also make the time to stop in and check in on their replacement, the one transitioning and the person assisting them with that transition.

Transitions do not only have to happen individually. You can have entire teams or organizations that go through transitions. The important thing to remember during a huge transition like this is that change is hard. Most people do not handle change well and change makes your team nervous, unbalanced, and unsure of themselves. If you want to transition and create or maintain a positive culture, then make sure you are staying extra transparent and available to your team. Encourage them to learn new processes and take part in the transition so they can build a sense of pride and ownership in the transition. Understand that not all teams or staff make it through transitions and be sensitive to that fact as well.

When you have a team or individuals who do not make it with you through a transition then be sensitive to the fact that you are negatively impacting someone's life. Just like corrective action, these decisions should not be made lightly or on a whim. They should not be knee-jerk reactions and should be handled delicately. In recent news, we learned that the Better.com CEO fired 900 employees over a Zoom call. While this might have seemed efficient to that leadership team it was very poorly handled. Even though these conversations take time the individuals must be treated as such, individuals.

While those conversations are uncomfortable, put yourself in their shoes, what would it be like to be so unceremoniously brushed off after all the hard work that you have put in? Take the time to walk into those meetings and give them the respect of a face-to-face conversation. Even if face to face means Zoom or Teams, turn your camera on, look them in the eye and tell them that their position has been eliminated. If possible, put together a good severance package so they can make it through another few paychecks and feed their families. If that means that your leadership team does without a bonus that year or they do not get their new office furniture, then so be it.

Another form of transition is to transition from one process to another. We are all guilty of spending months discussing a transition or process change and then halfway implementing it. Operationalize your processes and procedures, rules, and regulations so that they can be implemented across your organization. Make sure that all teams are made aware of changes so that they are all rowing in the same direction with the same understanding. When we transition from doing something one way to another way, we often find that there are those we forget to tell.

Those departments that maybe we don't interact with daily, or the person who was sick the day of the last leadership meeting. Unfortunately, I have seen leaders who have intentionally left other department heads out of transition decisions because they did not want to be questioned. They felt that it was no one else's business what they did with their department and that other department heads has no authority over them anyway. They have an attitude of "Well, I don't report to them, so I don't owe them anything." There we go with that insecurity and poor attitude again. The leaders and companies that succeed are the ones that know how to communicate and understand that the knowledge of many is always better than the knowledge of one.

Maybe that department head is not directly impacted by your decisions, but their staff could be. They could be handing out bad information to clients regarding your department believing that they are giving out accurate information. Set everyone around you up for success, not just yourself and not just your team. Transitions are things that the whole company should be aware of.

We should also be showing grace and be flexible when transitioning processes, rules, or organizational direction. Once we have communicated effectively to everyone, then we need to make sure everything is documented and rolled out cleanly. Once this takes place then we proactively reach out and check on the status. We cannot just roll out a new process and just turn and walk away and expect no bumps or hiccups. We need to proactively stay on top of the changes to make sure that the organization is not falling back into the habit of the old way of doing things. We need to allow the team time to absorb the new information, ask questions, provide training and practice.

Make sure you are not rolling out a half-baked idea. To prevent never-ending transitions make sure that you and the rest of the leadership team have completed and agreed upon the goals and purpose of the transition and that you are all on the same page before rolling it out on the floor. Stay in contact with each other and be willing to adjust if the reality of rolling out an idea does not quite line up with an original idea. Make sure that your teams are all comfortable and communicating any issues they are having transitioning in this new process so they can be corrected or handled right away.

Not all transitions have to be awful and impact lives. Most of them can be handled with poise and grace and, yes, leadership. When we stop and think through transitions we stop and take the time to consider every aspect of a position then we are ensuring that nothing is forgotten or left out. This prevents gaps in coverage or missed opportunities. It sets our teams and staff up for success and ensures that those leaving us are leaving us on the right foot. Impacting the lives of those around you is what leaders do daily. You get to choose whether that impact is positive or negative. As you have read throughout this book, leadership is never easy, but it is worth it.

Chapter 10
Proud Moments

Take a moment and look back at everything we have accomplished! We have defined what it is to be a leader, how to mentor a new leader, discussed being accountable, and talked about how to be more efficient with our time and people in our endless meetings. We discussed how to handle correction and development, develop a culture of positivity and success and how handle failure that will inevitably impact ourselves and our teams. We talked about building something that will outlive us and how to have a successful transition in our organization. This is a moment to be proud.

After the mentoring, you provide your young leaders, after taking all your energy and time to set them up for success step back and watch them work. This is the time to stand back and see what they can do. Have proud moments and share those with your young leaders and the leaders around you. One of the greatest compliments I feel I have ever received is one I was not even there for. My leader was in a meeting with the rest of the C-Suite and was presenting a report I had spent weeks preparing. When they complimented her on the report, she gave me my due by stating, "Thank you but Kailey put this report together. She has come a long way and has turned out to be the person I trust the most to handle things in my absence." She, of course, did not come and tell me she had said this. But a leader that I did not normally interact with, a C-Suite in fact, came into my office to compliment me on my report and filled me in on the compliment I had received.

I took a few moments and just allowed myself to feel the pride of a job well done. I had worked hard, held myself accountable, took ownership, and learned everything I could from anyone who would teach me. That led to my COO stating I was who they trusted most. Wow! What a compliment! The only compliment that beats that is the one I received about the person I was mentoring.

I spent months mentoring a manager, who had managed before but had never really been taught the how of leadership. I spent months doing one-on-ones, taking time every day to check on her and walk with her through any challenge she came up against. We discussed the team and I even stayed multiple evenings with her after work talking through the day and building report. A few months in we had grown to the point of needing a supervisor and we had moved a staff member from one team over to our team because of his excellent performance. In the time he was with us he had already exceeded everyone else in the department, was training new staff, and was assisting with projects as needed. Even though he was new we discussed bringing him on as a supervisor.

We decided to meet with him to discuss what the responsibilities would be if he was interested and what it would mean for him day in and day out. He was thrilled at the opportunity and jumped in with both feet. The first few months I spent with both manager and supervisor helping walk them through the why and how of leadership. I slowly began to take a step back and let the manager begin teaching the supervisor everything I had taught her. Within a few months, we were the most productive department and one of the smoothest operating departments.

During my one-on-one with the COO, she made a comment that I will never forget. She said, "You know I have one-on-ones with the other leaders. During those, I keep getting compliments on your manager and supervisor. Their professionalism and their reporting are great. I love the new reports that you are giving me every week, and everything seems to be going well on your team. Great job!" I was able to finally understand how my previous boss had felt when I was able to proudly say, "Thank you but my manager created those reports, and my supervisor built that process. I agree they are doing a great job and I will make sure to let them know."

What a proud mama moment! I was so excited that I almost flew back to my team and took great pleasure in watching the pride rush into their eyes and faces at the compliment. After that, they worked even harder and are now managers and directors at different organizations. While I do not work with one of them anymore, I still hear from them and talk through issues or situations that they have at the current organizations. The manager is now a director in my current organization and is the best mentor I have ever seen! It is a huge source of pride for me that I was able to help grow two individuals who stepped up to the plate with the right attitude and were sponges! They watched me succeed and watched me fail. We celebrated together, discussed life together, and even cried together. I mourned with them over personal loss and grief and celebrated with them when they succeeded in obtaining a new role or a promotion.

This is what proud moments are all about. Take the time to step back and look at all you and your teams have accomplished. Make a list every quarter if you need to! There is always more work to do and if we get stuck with our heads down and do not look up and take a breath now and again, we will get overwhelmed at the prospect of never being finished. If we do not stop to celebrate the victories and successes, we burn out and lose sight of why we do what we do.

Do that quarterly review for yourself and your team. Look back and help them celebrate the things they have accomplished every week, month, quarter, or year. Show them what they have been working so hard towards. Sometimes we can be running along with our head down thinking man, we will never reach that goal, when if we would just pick our head up, we would realize we had passed the goal six months ago. This is helpful on two fronts. Not only can you celebrate with your team all that you have accomplished, but you can also do a check-in to make sure that everything is still running smoothly.

As leaders, we tend to talk a lot about what should be done, spend a little time implementing it, and extraordinarily little time checking on it. If you are baking a cake and spent all this time preparing the ingredients, putting it in the right pans, setting the temperature, and then just walking away, all your arduous work will burn. You must check on it. Have you ever watched one of those baking competitions? You have these extraordinary artists in the kitchen who spend six hours rushing around trying to put something beautiful together and at the last second, they notice that their top cake is starting to cave into and sink into the cake below and with a sinking realization they remember they forgot to put in the support rods!

Don't let yourself and your team get to the end without doing a review to make sure you remembered to put in the support rods. Stop and take stock, be proud of what you have accomplished and find areas of opportunity to learn from it as well. Continuously improving yourself and your team is key. Remember the quote I live by? "Movement is life!" Keep moving and keep growing and you will always have something to be proud of.

"Success is a process for all of us, and as long as you are making consistent progress towards your goals—sincerely giving your best effort more often than not—then you are already successful and deserve to feel proud of yourself." - Hal Elrod

Hal here knows what he is talking about. Do not spend your career beating yourself up over the little things or forgetting to stop and see how far you have come, or you will spend your career in a frenzied state of never enough. Having a hunger to continuously grow does not mean that you cannot have proud moments of satisfaction to see where all you have come. In fact, taking the time to celebrate, and teaching your leaders to celebrate, will encourage them that much more to keep going! When you see the results of your hard work then you want to keep moving and see what else you can accomplish. So, take that time, step back, take a look, encourage your team and be a leader who knows how to appreciate success and have proud moments.

About the Author

KAILEY MARSHALL GREW UP IN A SMALL TOWN OUTSIDE OF DALLAS, WHERE she learned to have a strong work ethic from her parents. Growing up with horses, cows, and land to take care of, Kailey spent much of her childhood outside dreaming. It would not have been an odd occurrence to see Kailey pack up a backpack full of books and snacks and take off to go find a comfortable tree to spend the day reading and dreaming. Growing up, Kailey earned her first leadership position by the age of 20 and spent the next fourteen years gobbling up as much leadership advice as anyone would throw at her.

While working full-time Kailey decided to go back to school and completed her Bachelor of Science in Health Information Management and completed her MBA in Healthcare Management shortly after. She also obtained multiple certifications, including becoming a Registered Health Information Administrator, Certified Professional Coder, and Project Management Certifications. Kailey is also a proud member of the National Society of Leadership and Success, the American Association of Professional Coders, and the American Health Information Management Association.

Kailey's career has been mainly focused on healthcare and she has spent most of that time developing operational procedures, providing consultation services for physicians and facilities, and training and mentoring young leaders. Kailey currently resides in Texas.

www.ingramcontent.com/pod-product-compliance
Lightning Source LLC
Chambersburg PA
CBHW070301290526
45791CB00003B/1041